AUGUSTUS F. MOULTON

Grandfather Tales

of

Scarborough

OTHER BOOKS BY AUGUSTUS F. MOULTON

Trial by Ordeal

Sir Ferdinando Gorges and his Palatinate of Maine

Settlement of Scarborough

Anne Hutchinson

Church and State in New England

Moulton Family Genealogy

Old Prouts Neck

Grandfather Tales of Scarborough

by

Augustus F. Moulton

Foreword by

John Clair Minot

HERITAGE BOOKS
2012

HERITAGE BOOKS
AN IMPRINT OF HERITAGE BOOKS, INC.

Books, CDs, and more—Worldwide

For our listing of thousands of titles see our website
at
www.HeritageBooks.com

A Facsimile Reprint
Published 2012 by
HERITAGE BOOKS, INC.
Publishing Division
100 Railroad Ave. #104
Westminster, Maryland 21157

Copyright © 1925 Katahdin Publishing Company

— Publisher's Notice —
In reprints such as this, it is often not possible to remove blemishes from the original. We feel the contents of this book warrant its reissue despite these blemishes and hope you will agree and read it with pleasure.

International Standard Book Numbers
Paperbound: 978-0-7884-4129-5
Clothbound: 978-0-7884-9278-5

FOREWORD

LONG ago I served a joyous apprenticeship in newsgathering at Old Orchard. It was during the summer vacations of my college years at Bowdoin, and the Old Orchard of that halcyon era was not the Old Orchard of the present day—but that is another story. As a part of the routine of my job, particularly before the varied activities of the resort itself were in full swing, I used to ramble occasionally along that wonderful beach to Pine Point to gather up whatever stray items might seem worthy of publication in the Sea Shell the next day. And it never occurred to me to question that the name of Pine Point came from the whispering pines that grew down almost to the line where the surf came thundering in. It seemed as obvious as the name of Grand Beach close at hand.

Suddenly, and like making a great discovery, I have learned that the name goes back to that Charles Pine, a mysterious old pioneer who fought Indians there and felled great trees more than two centuries ago. He was a famous hunter, a hero of many daring adventures and an Indian fighter who helped make history in those brave days that the late 17th and early 18th centuries knew along the coast of Maine. How I regret that I had not heard about Charles Pine and his fellows in the years of those morning walks down the beach. What adventures the ready imagination of youth would have allowed me to enjoy with them! I loved local history even in those days, and had tried a boyish hand at writing some of it farther up the state. So it is that I feel somehow cheated because Mr. Moulton or some other historian had not put the story of early Scarboro before me at that time.

It is never too late. Scarboro has become quite another town since I have had the privilege of reading the galley proofs of the pages that follow. Hitherto it has been merely a town that was near Old Orchard—a pleasant town to ride through when *making the all too infrequent journey from a cluttered desk in Boston to the lake-encircled Kennebec town that is always home, though I have been there little enough in the past third of a century. I knew Scarboro as the birthplace of Maine's first governor and as a town that long suffered from a particularly virulent form of Democracy. I associated it with clams and salt marshes, with a meandering river and arching elms along the highway.*

Now it is all that, and so very much more. It is Old Black Point, Dunstan and Blue Point and Over the River. In its great forests where the wolves howl in winter, stand the giant pines with the mark of the broad R, that designates them as masts for the ships that will bear Drake and Nelson into battle a thousand leagues away. It is the home of those wonderful pioneer women, Margaret Cammock, Eleanor Bailey and Elizabeth Dearing. It is peopled by the Strattons, the Prouts, the Pines, the Algers and all the others who subdue the wilderness and stand siege against the raiding redmen. It knows again the settlers who build the mills that will vanish, the houses of worship that will disappear, the homes of which even the cellars will be hard to find and the highways that will be abandoned. It is the town that rivals Portland in population and importance as America's independence becomes a dream realized. It is, in short, all that it has been through the centuries—so truly does the past live in Mr. Moulton's pages.

How absurd it is to speak of the past as dead! All the life that fires the present comes from the spark that the deathless past has loaned us. All that we have or are is due to the bounty of that past which is not dead, which is not left behind us at all, but which leaps along at our stirrup wherever we ride through the tangled paths of the present.

Mr. Moulton has done his task supremely well. Combining his ripe scholarship and his capacity for historical research with the tales and traditions handed down in his family, he has given us a local history that is beyond price. Particularly, his chapters on the early proprietors and on the origins of the land titles are of much value in the case of numerous Maine towns. It is a work to be treasured far beyond the circle of those who have Scarboro blood in their veins.

Local history may be handled in many ways. Gorham, for example, is forever fortunate that Elijah Kellogg has put the story of its first settlers into his "Good Old Times." Mr. Moulton has been happy in giving a touch of romance to his historical work. The result is no less accurate than the local history that follows the conventional formula, and assuredly it is vastly more readable. There are yet a hundred Maine towns that need such a work as Mr. Moulton has done for Scarboro—and it is a work that cannot well be long delayed. True, not many of them have roots so far into the past as those of old Scarboro, and few are so rich in historical material; but in the case of each town there are those who love it well, and the future will be the poorer for all the sons and daughters of Maine if any single town is neglected by the historian whose heart is really in the old days and who cherishes all the romance that lives forever in them.

JOHN CLAIR MINOT.

CONTENTS

	PAGE
My Grandfather	3
The Fabyans and the Millikens	11
The Stuart Brook	15
Ezra Carter Homestead	21
Roads and Highways	25
The Movement for Better Highways	31
Dunstan of the Alger Settlement	39
The Scarboro Marshes and the Dyke	45
The Rivers and the Old Seaport	51
The Shipping and the Shipyard	57
The King Family and Resident People	65
Old Dunstan Corner	75
Old Times in the Vicinity	81
Taverns and Stage Coaches	87
Over the River District	95
Charles Pine and the Pioneer Settlers	101
Random Grandfather Tales	109
The Indian Wars and Garrison Houses	119
Black Point and Prouts Neck	129
The Prouts Neck Title	139
The Churches and Parishes	145
How the Old Orthodox Church Became Unpopular	157
Schools and Educational System	167
Social Customs and Neighborhood Affairs	175
The Proprietors of Scarborough	185
Individual Ownership of Land in America	199
Three Scarboro Women	207

Grandfather Tales

of

Scarborough

The Grandfather, Ezra Carter

Grandfather Tales

OF SCARBOROUGH

I

MY GRANDFATHER

MY grandfather on my mother's side was Ezra Carter, son of Ezra and Phebe Whittemore Carter and grandson of Daniel and Hannah Fowler Carter of Concord, N. H. He was born in Concord March 18, 1773; came to Scarboro to reside about the year 1800. He had, as he said, only a few months of schooling, but was a great reader and wrote a good hand and was an exceptionally well informed man. After attaining his majority, he learned the trade of tanner with Captain Richard Ayer of Concord. Then, as he expressed it, he took a cruise through Maine and spent a summer working at Wiscasset. He was a vigorous youth and was never thrown, he said, in a wrestling match. His sister, Hannah, had married Parson Edmund Eastman of Limerick, Maine, who appears to have been temporarily at the Second Parish, Dunstan, Church, and Ezra made a visit to his sister there. Squire Joshua Fabyan was then one of the active business men of Scarboro and a prominent man in the community. He had been in the Revolutionary days Tax Commissioner for the District of Maine, and helped to raise a regiment. He had also been a member of the Massachusetts General Court, and was one of the Justices of the Court of Common Sessions and was one of the first Overseers of the new Bowdoin College. The Fabyans prior to 1730, while the Indians were still skulking about, took up a large tract of land in Scarboro, Southerly of Dunstan, on the North Westerly side of the Portland and Saco highway.

The Grandfather Ezra Carter Homestead

MY GRANDFATHER

Squire Joshua lived on the old Fabyan homestead. This was afterwards occupied by his son, Joshua, who married Mary Downing of Kennebunk, and next by Joshua's son, Squire John Downing Fabyan and later by Martha Ann Fabyan, daughter of John D. One Simeon Fitts was his adjoining neighbor, owning a large farm on the Southerly side towards Saco. The Fitts farm was then in Scarboro, the town line being about three-quarters of a mile Southwest of its present location as established by setting off a part of old Scarboro to Saco in 1841.

While visiting his sister Hannah Eastman, Ezra Carter met Sally Fabyan, the daughter of Squire Joshua, and they were married at Scarboro, October 2, 1797. Parson Edmund Eastman became pastor of the church at Limerick, and lived there a good many years. He was a Harvard man and was instrumental in founding Limerick Academy. Ezra Carter and his young wife established themselves first in Limerick, where he set himself up as a tanner, a business in which he took great pride, and later used to tell of kindly relations with Friend Josiah Dow, the father of Neal Dow of Portland, also a tanner. At Limerick the oldest child, Joseph Fabyan, was born December 11, 1798 and likewise the second child, Sarah Brackett, born September 30, 1800 and named for her maternal grandmother Sarah, daughter of Anthony Brackett of Portland. Squire Joshua Fabyan died in Scarboro June 20, 1799, and Ezra Carter and his wife soon after moved from Limerick to the Fabyan homestead.

Simeon Fitts, the neighbor on the Southwesterly side, seems to have died without direct heirs and his will was said to have been "broken" so that his big farm was divided among a lot of distant relatives. My grandfather enlarged his original Fabyan purchase by acquiring several portions or strips from the heirs, and thus increased his home place to about seventy-five acres. He also bought a wood lot of some 18 acres on the old Blue

FREEDOM MOULTON
FATHER OF AUGUSTUS F. MOULTON

MY GRANDFATHER

Point road for "a good harness and a ten-dollar bill" and this developed into a valuable tract of timber. He, however, always devoted himself to his tannery and did but little farming. He lived on the homestead where the big elms stand, until he died March 10, 1868 at the age of 95. His oldest son, Joseph Fabyan Carter, lived with him there and they carried on the tannery until about 1850, when Fabyan, as he was called, got the Western fever and moved with his family to Dover, Illinois. Then the youngest son, Ilus Fabyan Carter, who had been in business in New York City, took the tannery and put in new machinery with a windmill and enlargement. The business was not very prosperous and in 1853 the place was transferred to my father, Freedom Moulton. He was son of Captain Joshua who lived "over the river" as the part of the town above the Nonsuch River was called, and had fitted for but did not go to Bowdoin College. For several years he taught the Dunstan School Winter and Summer and boarded at the Carter homestead. He married my mother, Shuah Coffin Carter, and they went to Jay in Franklin County, in 1842 and lived there until he bought the Carter place and tannery in 1853. He did not continue the tannery, but taught school and managed the farm until he died in 1857. He was a Justice of the Peace, an Ensign in the State Militia, and was Town Clerk of Scarboro at the time of his decease.

I was something less than five years old when they took up their residence on the old place, and my grandfather and I were quite like boon companions. The old gentleman read his Bible through consecutively at least once a year and diligently read his New Testament and Psalms every day. He was a most interesting talker and loved to tell of the old times and the old traditions. Hunting and trapping foxes seemed to have been his recreation winters when he was not occupied with the tannery, and apparently he remembered every individual fox that he had captured. He keenly enjoyed telling of testing the wit of himself and his dog against the marvelous cunning of the fox.

I remember many things that he related about the early settlers and the early settlement. The town lands away from the sea-shore were not taken up to any great extent until the Indian troubles ceased, and there were hostile Indians lurking around until after 1720. "The old fox," Sebastian Rale, was slain and his outpost at Norridgewock broken up in 1724. After that time the danger in Scarboro from the Indians and the French, who incited them to hostility, seems pretty much to have ceased, though murderous raids were made in various places until Quebec was captured in 1759. Great sections of forest and farming lands were taken up, saw-mills were built on almost every stream and the upper parts of the town quite rapidly became settled. The limits of these tracts were not well defined and disputes about boundary lines were common.

II

The Fabyans and the Millikens

II

THE FABYANS AND THE MILLIKENS

ONE of the earliest of my grandfather's tales that I remember was the contention of the Fabyans and the Millikens about their division line. The land grants had commonly been in large tracts with uncertain limits. Naturally, he was chiefly interested in the Fabyan side. The Millikens who owned lands Southeasterly of the Fabyan territory, on the other side of the Saco and Portland road, were descendants of the Algers who established the original Dunstan settlement, about 1651, and which was abandoned upon the French invasion of 1690. The Fabyans and the Millikens were rival mill owners on the brook which ran through the lands of both. The dividing line between their holdings was a subject of dispute. The Fabyans' Southeasterly line, bounding on the Milliken tract, as my grandfather said, was given as sixty poles above "the great falls" on the brook. There are on this brook three sets of falls, all then available for mill privileges. The Fabyans claimed the boundary as sixty rods above the lower falls, sometimes called Blackman's Falls, which are manifestly greater than the others, while the Millikens claimed the middle falls, which they asserted were "the great falls," as the starting point. The Milliken claim would have given them all of the mill privileges on the brook. The Fabyans had and retained possession of the land which included the upper fall, but placed their buildings to the Northwest of the highway and far enough from it to be beyond the disputed line. The elms planted about the original homestead have grown into very large trees, but the apple trees which they set out as a part of the ornamental row there, are gone.

There were two Fabyan immigrants to Scarboro, Captain John, unmarried and rough in manners, and Joseph, one of the founders of the Second Parish Church, a man of mild and gentle disposition. They were connected with the Bracketts and came from Newington, N. H., first to Portland, then to Scarboro some time after the year 1727, the date of their first deed. Both were buried in the Fabyan graveyard on their farm and were later removed to the Dunstan Cemetery. Captain John was belligerent and always ready to maintain what he believed to be his rights. The old gentleman said that the Millikens once had a surveyor to run out, according to their claim, the disputed division line between them and the Fabyans, and the rough Captain John went out and smashed the compass with his broad-axe and drove them off. His fighting weight was just what he weighed any minute, and, without much help from his meeker brother, they won out and held their bigness of territory in spite of opposition, but there always remained a traditional tinge of hostility between the Fabyans and the Millikens.

III

The Stuart Brook

Grandfather Home and Stuart Brook

III

THE STUART BROOK

THE brook on which the three sets of falls are located, my grandfather said, was in the earlier times much larger than now appears and was called the Western River in the Alger Indian deed. The cutting off of the forests dried up the springs and reduced its size. I never heard any particular name given regularly to this brook. The lower sections of it were often called by the name of the owner of the territory through which it flowed. It was, however, I think, in its entirety quite generally known as the Stuart Brook, its source being on land of the Stuarts who had another large tract to the westward. Before the thick trees were cleared away, it must have been a stream of no inconsiderable size. There are two branches about a mile above, but the Stuart Brook is throughout the main stream.

On this brook, at the upper falls just Northwest of the present Portland and Saco road, which was the old highway to Portsmouth and Boston, was located the Fabyan saw-mill. The little pond made by the plunge of water from

GREAT FALLS ON STUART BROOK

the flume which turned the mill wheel is still plainly apparent, as is also the graded roadway to the mill on the Northerly side. This Fabyan mill, though it had no great fall, had by far the most ample mill pond and had also the first use of the water. The mill pond extended a long way up the stream and in the bed of the brook there are still sunken logs. It was also a resort for wild water fowl.

My grandfather pointed out to me the sites of four mills on this stream. First above was the Fabyan saw-mill at the upper fall, then at the middle fall below, there was a grist-mill. The circular granite mill stone used in the mill rested on the bank nearby until recently. Near the gristmill and probably connected with it, was also a cloth mill or "fulling-mill," so called, for carding wool and "fulling" cloth. This mill was always embarrassed by its limited mill pond. At the lower falls was the Milliken saw-mill. The water there makes a double descent of some twenty-five feet and the power was strong. Old slabs and logs still encumber the broad pool, washed out by the water which poured over the dam and then down the side of the precipice. In the Spring freshets, the water still rushes over these falls with quite impressive volume and roar. Below this Milliken waterfall, large speckled sea trout are sometimes caught, but there are no trout above. The brook flows through the meadows below and that part was sometimes called Milliken's brook. It unites with the stream which comes from the Cascade Falls, so called, on the Old Foxwell's Brook. This Foxwell stream is said to have its source at the Great Heath and in its course crosses the Portland and Saco road and also the Old Orchard road, and is the "Leaping Brook" of Whittier's poem of Mogg Megone. The Stuart Brook which turned the wheels of the Fabyan and Milliken mills flows, after its junction with the Foxwell Brook, by a winding course to Dunstan Landing. It should be noted that in its lower part this brook was subject to tidal flow, so it is not surprising that it was called by the Algers, the Western River.

Just where the old Blue Point road crosses the augmented Foxwell's Brook or Western River was, as I have been told, the place where Richard King built his saw-mill when he first came to Scarboro in 1744. The mill dam was constructed mostly of earth taken from the roadway of the old road to Blue Point as is plainly shown by the extensive excavation of the highway track leading Northwesterly, and the travelled way now follows the crest of the curving dam of King's Mill to and across the present bridge. Richard King's house is said to have been located upon the high ground near by, just Westerly of the point where the electric car track leaves the highway. The cellar of the house is plainly apparent and English made bricks may be found there. The mill itself was on the Northeasterly side of the road about at the ledge close by the present bridge. This was called Tyler's bridge from one Tyler who lived there, and it had about the location of the ancient Henry Watts saw-mill during the first settlement, near which Southeasterly was the residence of one John Moulton from Hampton, N. H. Richard King afterward moved to Dunstan Landing where he had a store and shipped great quantities of lumber and masts to England and the West Indies.

THE GRANDFATHER HOME, SCARBORO

IV

Ezra Carter Homestead

IV

EZRA CARTER HOMESTEAD

THE Fabyan saw-mill, which has been mentioned as located West of the Portland and Saco road, appears to have gone out of commission about the time Squire Joshua Fabyan died and Ezra Carter and Sally Fabyan, his wife, moved to the Fabyan homestead in Scarboro. The original Fabyan house was situated somewhat Southerly from, but quite near the location of, the house now standing there. This present two-story house was built by my grandfather, Ezra Carter, about 1815. The old Fabyan house to which he came was the second dwelling house built upon the location, the first having been destroyed by the great fire of 1762 which swept over nearly all the western part of the town from Saco to the Nonsuch River. The big elms standing in front of the Carter place now owned by Abbott are irregular in spacing because apple trees were set out as part of the row. Some of these apple trees lived more than a hundred years and died of old age. The Joshua Fabyan who was son of Squire Joshua and married Mary Downing, lived some ten rods easterly of the conspicuous big elms which stood in front of the old Fabyan-Carter homestead. The younger Joshua built there a new two-story house connected with two barns. The buildings erected by him were struck by lightning and wholly destroyed a few years ago. There is nothing left to show the location except some balm of gilead trees.

John Fabyan, son of Joseph and brother of Squire Joshua, lived some distance farther eastwardly toward Dunstan, about where the elm trees near the Joseph C. Snow house now stand. This John sold out and moved to Leeds, Maine. One of his sons was Horace Fabyan, a hotel man who established the Fabyan House at the White Mountains. When Ezra Carter in

1815 built the two-story house now standing, its predecessor, the old Fabyan House rebuilt after the fire and the same occupied by Squire Joshua, was moved to Dunstan Landing where it still stands. It was occupied as a dwelling house by Frederick Milliken and after him by his son Samuel K. Milliken. My grandfather's new house was put together wholly with hand-wrought nails. Even the shingle nails were hand-made. The lumber used was mostly the old growth "punkin pine" with big hewn beams and rafters and boards wide enough for wainscoting.

Ezra Carter established a tannery first upon the location of the old saw-mill, or perhaps it was the old saw-mill remodeled. It had pits in which leather was made by steeping the hides for several months in vats filled with wet hemlock bark, and was quite near to the present Westerly side line of the Portland and Saco road. This county road was originally irregular with many crooks and turns and was widened and straightened about the year 1829. The change of the highway to the West when the road was widened and straightened made it necessary for grandfather to remove his tan yard, which he did to a place up the brook near his house. The new tannery was a long building with a tan yard in front near the brook; a windmill was attached but was not reliable and the hemlock bark was ground by horse power.

V

Roads and Highways

V

ROADS AND HIGHWAYS

THE change of the highway location and the removal of the tannery suggests the extended movement for improving the highways in the early part of the century.

In the colony times my grandfather said the roads were little more than trails or bridle paths with no recorded limits. Wheeled vehicles for driving purposes were practically unknown. Horseback riding was the regular thing, women riding on pillions behind the men. The roads were used mostly by ox teams with heavy loads and teaming was done largely on the snow in winter.

It is not possible to give with certainty the locations of the ancient roads, for the trails followed generally the firm and available ground rather than any direct course, avoiding so far as possible the swamps and hills. The old road to Blue Point left the Saco road at Capt. Mulbury Milliken's tavern, being practically a continuance of the Fabyan mill road or lane, and followed the hill crest Easterly in line with Stuart brook past the lower falls, then continued through the woods to the Richard King residence and mill on the Foxwell brook or "Western River" and crossing at Tyler's bridge. A little beyond, it turned quite abruptly to the left, avoiding the low land on the one side and the swamp on the other, then after quite a distance it swung around at a sharp angle to the right and continued up and over the Blue Point hill, connecting with the Seavey's Landing road or trail.

There are still traces of an old road across the Fabyan territory beginning at the Boston and Portland highway near the John Fabyan—the present Joseph C. Snow—house, and taking its crooked course Westerly to the Stuart neighborhood and to what is called the Flag Pond. The apple trees in the orchard at the Carter and Fabyan places were set out to correspond with the line of this road and that is the reason why the rows of trees are at angles with the present farm fence lines. The Stuart houses were on this old road about two miles away and the children from that section used it in going to the Dunstan School. The discontinuance of the road left the Stuart residences at some distance from the newer main highway called the Woods road. The Joshua Fabyan referred to, son of Squire Joshua, I was told, lived for a while in the cleared field just across the Stuart brook nearly a mile to the westward where there are many old apple trees. This field I have heard called the Eli Seavey or Fogg field. The cellar of the house may still be located there and daffodils and old-fashioned flowers bloom in the grass where once was the front yard.

The old travelled way from Dunstan to Portland the old gentleman described as turning off Northerly just beyond the Broad Turn road and going past the Southgate or Alger falls and the mill location on Alger's brook, which lower down is called Old House Creek, then continuing Westerly across present pasture land and woods, skirting the marshes, to the Graffam and Burnham houses, then swinging Northerly across the meadow it made a steep climb straight up Scottow's Hill. Down the hill on the other side it turned Southeasterly to about the present county road location, then going Northeasterly past the old Moses mill on Mill Creek it continued over Oak Hill and across the Nonsuch River and at a considerable distance beyond went Northerly past the present State Reform School and thence wandered on to the bridge across the Stroudwater River, and then on to Portland. It was exceedingly crooked, making of it a long route. When pensions were granted to the soldiers of 1812, they were allowed for two days time going on foot from Dunstan to Portland. Winding and irregular as this was, it was much more direct than the earlier route.

In considering the road systems of the lower part of the town, one must take into account the extensive marshes with crooked streams, subject for quite a distance above Dunstan to the ebb and flow of the tide. The tidal rise and fall is nearly ten feet, so that the Owascoag and other streams that unite into the estuary called Scarboro River were often overflowingly full at high water, and the marsh and water ways that divided the town into the first and second parishes were quite impassable without boats. The town lines were established by measurements on the sea frontage before the interior had been much explored and ran due Southeast and Northwest.

Parting of the Ways—Prouts Neck

VI

The Movement for Better Highways

VI

THE MOVEMENT FOR BETTER HIGHWAYS

ACCORDING to the first U. S. Census taken in 1790 Portland had 2246 inhabitants, while Scarboro numbered 2235. Under the stimulus given to American Shipping after the Revolution and the wars of Napoleon, Portland, which had been burned by Mowatt in 1775, grew up fast. Stage coach lines were established between Portland and Portsmouth, then to Boston soon after the close of the Revolutionary War.

The Portland road was especially crooked and bad. It was helped a little by a causeway and bridge across the marsh Southwesterly of Scottow's Hill, cutting out the long loop there. That part of the road between the Sewall Milliken and Ira Milliken places is still called The Causeway.

In 1799, the Court of Common Sessions ordered an alteration of the road over Scottow's Hill so that it should go around the base of the hill instead of straight over the top. Before this order was carried out a corporation was, in 1801, chartered by the Massachusetts legislature to build a turnpike road from the bridge near the Nat. Moses place Southwesterly straight across the marsh to Robert Southgate's and to meet the county road South of the Second Parish meeting-house at Dunstan. This company, of which old Judge Robert Southgate was chief manager, built the present turnpike road across the marsh. The alteration around Scottow's Hill was revoked. Vaughn's toll bridge, entering Portland, was built at about the same time and a pretty direct route was thus opened, but was subject to the payment of tolls at the turnpike and bridge.

In 1815 the Payne road was laid out, following almost a straight course from where the old Portland road, so called, makes a turn to go over Scottow's Hill and extending in direct line to the bridge at Stroudwater. (See Court of Common

Sessions records, Vol. 3, Page 271.) It is said to have received its name from one Payne, a stage driver, who took an active part in its establishment.

The Boston highway crossing of the Stuart-Fabyan-Milliken brook referred to was then just Easterly of the present location and was especially difficult. One Daniel Granger of the stage line in 1829 headed a movement which brought about an application to the Court of Common Sessions to widen and straighten the Boston-Portland highway and this made necessary the raising of the grade and building a new bridge over the Stuart Brook Westerly of the old bridge location. It was this change of grade that injured the access to the Carter tannery and compelled its removal. Mr. Carter received an award of five dollars for his land damage, which award was later increased to eleven dollars, but the old gentleman always considered that he was badly used, as he was put to large expense in constructing a new tan yard and erecting new buildings just Southerly of his dwelling house.

The new road connecting with the turnpike was laid out through the old Second Parish meeting-house lot, so called, at Dunstan, taking most of it, but leaving the portion upon which the soldiers monument now stands. The Turnpike had its gate and toll gatherer until about 1855 when that and Vaughn's Bridge were taken over by the County and made free travel. The gravel for the Scarboro Pike was taken mostly from the deep ground pit opposite the old Dunstan school-house lot on the hill.

All the old highways in this vicinity up to about 1800 were very crooked and difficult for passage. A good many became disused and abandoned after the movement for better roads began and the routes of travel were straightened and in many cases newly located. This is the reason for finding occasional groups of houses like those of the Stuarts and of the Graffam-

THE MOVEMENT FOR BETTER HIGHWAYS

Burnham settlement "in from the road." The main road from Portland to Saco originally wound about so that the Uncle Nathaniel Boothby farm buildings Southwest of the Saco line later occupied by his son Benjamin and after him by his grandson George H. which were then in Scarboro, were on its Westerly side instead of easterly as at present. The general straightening, widening and relocating of the roads was regarded by many as quite unnecessary, and the towns had to be spurred into taking action by frequent complaints to the courts and by indictments and fines. When the stage coaches came with their galloping horses they appeared to the staid and older people to be reckless and extravagant methods of travel.

There were in the early part of the century very few wheel vehicles except ox rigging for carrying loads. My grandfather had one of the first riding wagons built. It was quite ornate and was serviceable both for general driving and for carrying leather. After lighter vehicles came into use he put this wagon body into the cellar as a receptacle for vegetables. When heaping full it would hold more than fifteen bushels of potatoes. The axles of heavy carts were generally of wood. Iron appears to have been used rather sparingly. In the old Fabyan barn was preserved for many years a wooden plow covered on the outside with strips of wrought iron. Cooking stoves were unknown and brick ovens for the weekly baking day and the Dutch ovens, a movable contrivance, were reckoned as great improvements. The lucifer friction match made a revolution in lighting fires.

Somewhere about 1840, after the Portland and Saco and Portsmouth railroad was built, a new road was laid out Southerly from the Saco road near the Dunstan school-house, connecting with the old Blue Point road for the better convenience of the Dunstan people going to the new railroad depot located at the crossing of this road. The new branch is the one now used and contains the track of the electric road. It crosses "Drunken Gully," so called on account of the excessive consumption of "spirits" when the bridge there was under construction. Just at the point where the new road entered the old, and on its Westerly side, is still to be seen traces of the foundation of a house which was long occupied by Johnny Dearborn, a Revolutionary soldier. There was also a traveled road extending Northeasterly from this point through the woods to Dunstan Landing on which was a house of one Patterson.

The slowness and difficulty of travel gave occasion for numerous taverns for the entertainment and refreshment of wayfarers. The Millikens, before they built the present brick house on the Saco road, had there a tavern called Mulberry's tavern with a stable on the opposite side for horses and oxen. The Milliken occupants of this spot, according to my grandfather's recollection, were Capt. Mulbury Milliken, then his son, Capt. Benjamin Milliken, and after him Dr. John Mulbury Milliken, son of Benjamin, who was for a long time a well known country doctor. Dr. John in my recollection carried on the big farm in a very skilful manner.

Frequent inquiry is made concerning the location of the ancient highways. It is not possible, however, to give with any degree of exactness the old routes of travel. They were in general only common pathways, following the firm and available ground rather than any direct course, avoiding so far as possible the swamps and hills and seeking fords across streams. It was often easier to climb straight over an elevation than to go around it. The ancient tracks were also constantly changing, as few of them until later times had any official location. The town now has a pretty good system of roads and highways, following in most cases the general direction of early routes, straightened and defined and eliminating so far as possible the abrupt crooks and windings. Many portions have been discontinued and additions made to give a more direct course and entirely new lines of travel laid out. Traces of what were common ways of travel may be found almost anywhere and not a few have become public ways by long usage.

JUDGE ROBERT SOUTHGATE MANSION—DUNSTAN

Shell Heaps—Winnock's Neck

VII

Dunstan of the Alger Settlement

VII

DUNSTAN OF THE ALGER SETTLEMENT

THE old gentleman used to speak of Dunstan as a place of no small importance in former times, though with the coming of railways and the falling off of local water transportation and stage coaches, its growth and prominence mostly disappeared. The present name is probably a misnomer. The Algers, Andrew and Arthur, who made the original settlement there came, according to James P. Baxter's quite minute account, from Dunster, an ancient place near the Bristol Channel in Southwestern England. This is in Somerset County, though so near the Devonshire coast, noted for adventurous seamen, that people from that region were commonly called Devonshire men. The red cattle of New England were mainly of the Devonshire stock. The general appearance of the locality with the marshes and with the conspicuous Scottow's Hill adjacent is quite suggestive of the English Dunster. The new-comers frequently named their establishments for places in the old country, and we find many transported names like as Biddeford, Scarborough, Stroudwater and Falmouth.

Dunstan, which name included the village and the landing at the river half a mile away Southeasterly, was part of the large Alger tract. This tract, according to declaration of Uphannum, otherwise Jane the Indian, recorded in York records of date 1659, was purchased by the two Algers in 1651 of her father, the Sagamore, her mother, her brother and herself. The bounds began at the place still called "The Partings" where the river, called in Indian, Owascoag, unites with the "Blew Point" River (called later Scarborough River), and extended on the one side Northerly by that "Northermost river that dreaneth by the great hill of Abram Jocelyn," namely the said Owascoag, up to the place afterwards called Rice's bridge, which apparently was at the head of its tidal flow. On the other side, starting from the same "Partings" it follows up the serpentine course of the Scarboro or old Dunstan River Southerly and Southwesterly, past the bend at Dunstan Landing, and going on Southwesterly continued up by what was called the Western River to its meeting with Foxwell's Brook, and then by a sharp turn Northwesterly and keeping the course of this Western River, called later in its upper portion the Stuart Brook, to a point sixty poles above the Great Falls of the brook. The Northwesterly bound, stated in reverse, was a line with angles, extending S. W. from the first named stopping point on the Northernmost (Owascoag) River, just beyond Scottow's Hill back to the point of limit on the Western River, or Stuart Brook. The Fabyan lands, therefore, were bounded Southeasterly upon the Alger tract.

As the tide then flowed nearly up to the Great Falls of the Stuart Brook, the part below might well be called a river. It was the point of termination of the "sixty pooles" above the Great Falls, being according to the Fabyan claim just at the present location of the Portland and Saco road, that gave rise to the later controversy between the Millikens and the Fabyans. Old people related the tradition that the size of the Alger purchase was, so much as a man could walk around in half a summer day. The actual survey was not made for many years after the date of the Indian deed.

The Algers established a considerable settlement at Dunstan, but both lost their lives, and the place was temporarily abandoned, at the outbreak of the Indian War in 1675. In the French-Indian attack in 1690, all the settlers were driven off, and the place was wholly deserted for a dozen years or more. After the wars were over some former residents returned, and with them new-comers, and took possession of lots for themselves.

The heirs of John Milliken of Boston, who married Elizabeth Alger, revived their claim of ownership of the Alger territory under the Indian deed. This was a long time after. Some of the Millikens were living on farms there, and in accordance with a petition in the Supreme Judicial Court at Boston, for a legal partition of the lands of the Milliken heirs, an excellent delineation of the whole locality was made by Moses Banks in 1784. This plan is recorded in Cumberland Registry

THE OLD CANAL—DUNSTAN LANDING

of Deeds, Book 100, Page 570. It conforms to the Fabyan boundary claim, and is supplemented by a deposition of James Springer, recorded in Book 103, Page 313, relating to the occupation of the premises. Springer says he came to Scarboro in 1728, and was with John Jones in 1730 when he ran the lines, and that he knew of the Milliken occupation.

This is a good example of title by Indian deeds. The roving aborigines had no more idea of individual ownership of land than the birds or the foxes, but the description in the Indian deed gave boundaries for the tract which the grantee might claim he was holding and occupying. In this way title by possession was obtained, the Sagamore deed giving bounds and so called color of title, and the occupation, by virtue of the statute, ripening into ownership.

On the Northeasterly side of the road from the village to Dunstan Landing, called the Landing Road, near the ravine which leads Easterly down to the marsh, is the reputed location of the Alger houses. This assertion regarding location has little support further than the finding of charred wood and grain there, coupled with the fact that the houses of the Algers and others were burned in the Indian attack of 1675, when one of the brothers was killed and the other mortally wounded. As communication was then chiefly by water, a location at some distance from the boat landing place would seem to have been inconvenient.

Horatio Hight was sure from other references that the Algers' cabins stood just Northwesterly of the bridge on the Saco and Portland turnpike road over the little stream known as Old House Creek, or Alger's Creek, as it is also called. At the bend of the stream, near the short Milliken road, there is a very favorable landing place and a spring and sheltered building spot. Both statements may be correct, as the houses of the brothers and others were quite likely at some distance apart. Before the sudden attack, a considerable number of people had been living there for about twenty years, all the time at peace and friendship with the natives.

VIII

The Scarboro Marshes and the Dyke

ACROSS THE MARSHES FROM NEAR THE DEPOT—PINE POINT

VIII

THE SCARBORO MARSHES AND THE DYKE

HE marshes were a very valuable asset in the early times. They produced large crops of hay which, though somewhat salt, furnished winter support for the cattle. No cultivation was required. It could be cut and stacked on "staddles" to keep it above the flow of high tides, and taken to the home barns on the first snow. Sometimes it was loaded on gundalows and floated to the Landing, and there cured and hauled away in the summer. Another attraction existed in the fish and sea fowl, native and migratory, which were there in an abundance that can scarcely be comprehended at the present time. A large part of the upper marshes belonged, after the second settlement, to Richard King, and from him came to the Southgates. When Judge Horatio Southgate, who was the son of Dr. Robert and the last of the name in Scarboro, died about 1864, all his real estate was sold to Ezra Carter, Jr., son of my grandfather and Seth Scamman of Saco.

Curiously enough the building of the extension to Portland of the Boston and Maine Railroad, was a potent factor in shutting off the sea tides from the marshes. In 1871 an old-fashioned railroad contest had arisen between the Eastern and the Boston and Maine Railroads. The railway connection between Portland and Boston had first consisted of a separate company, the Portland, Saco & Portsmouth Railroad, which extended from Portland to Portsmouth, where it made connection with Boston by the line of the Eastern Railroad. The Boston and Maine was a separate road, beginning at the P. S. & P. at North Berwick, making it from that place a competitor of the Eastern Railroad. The Eastern came under the management of reckless financiers, who got control of the P. S. & P. road and attempted to exclude the Boston and Maine from through connection with Portland. The result was that the

Boston and Maine got a charter in 1871 and built the new branch from North Berwick to Portland. In consideration for building the long bridge across the mouth of Scarborough River without a draw, the Boston and Maine Railroad paid the town partly enough to construct a new road across the marsh from Blue Point to Pine Point, and another new road was built from Dunstan Landing to a connection with the old Blue Point road. Pine Point had been quite inaccessible, except by water, and had then become a deserted region, a resort for wild fowl and a nesting place for crows. The new highway opened it up, giving a direct road from Dunstan to the sea, and made of it a summer resort.

In 1876 a company was formed to build a dyke wall to shut out the tide water from the marshes above the P. S. & P., then controlled by the Eastern Railroad. The chief promoter of the dyking project was Seth Scamman, who with Ezra Carter, Jr. had bought the Southgate property with its great area of salt marsh. The dyking company was chartered by the State Legislature and authorized to construct the dyke and dam and levy a tax for payment upon the land of the owners benefited. This it did with a long dyke wall of its own above the railroad. The business management of the Company was poor, the construction work inferior and the result a disappointment. For a couple of years the production of grass upon the drained land was phenomenal, and the quality of the hay was excellent, then the peaty surface dried up and a great part became little better than a barren waste. The Company failed, owners would not pay their assessments and the promoters were large losers. After a while the Eastern Railroad consented to put in a tide gate in their bridge, in consideration of the discontinuance of the draw-bridge over the Dunstan or Scarboro River, which had long been maintained, though used but little. In process of time there has been considerable of improvement in the quality

of the dyked land. This exclusion of water communication with
the ocean, with its big majestic tidal flow, has vastly altered the
appearance of the locality. Before that, at flood tide it made an
imposing appearance.

GARRISON COVE—PROUTS NECK

IX

The Rivers and the Old Seaport

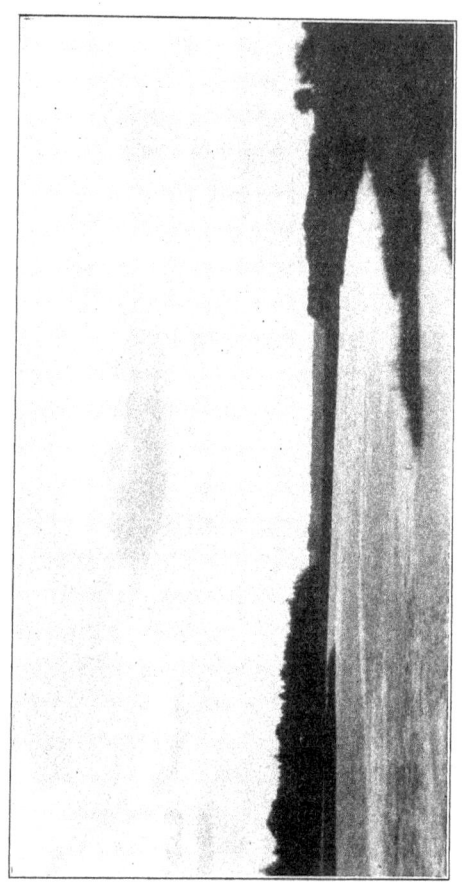

View of the Spurwink River Between Scarboro and Cape Elizabeth

IX

THE RIVERS AND THE OLD SEAPORT

HE rivers, which take their seaward way by very winding courses through the level marshes, seem to have had no permanently established names. At what part of the Old River the name of Scarborough applies, it is difficult to say. At the Landing and below it was often referred to as the Dunstan River. In the Alger Indian deed, its upper course Westerly from the starting point at "the partings," meaning the inflow entrance of Old House Creek, and following up what we call the Stuart Brook, is referred to as "the Western River." Below the landing it received the addition of Old House or Alger's Creek and the Owascoag River and other streams as it went along. Perhaps the term, Scarborough, applies with substantial correctness to all the old lower part from Dunstan Landing to the sea. After the main stream receives the waters of Libby's River and the Nonsuch, some three miles below, it becomes a broad estuary. Being subject to ocean tides it was at the period of high water twice a day brimming full from bank to bank and often overflowing upon the marshes. At flood tide it would float what were in the old times considered large vessels, having probably a depth of some fifteen feet.

Dunstan, which name included both Landing and the village half a mile away was, up to the time of the Revolution and after, quite an important seaport. Fish, dried and pickled, and especially lumber, were carried in ships directly to England and the West Indies and elsewhere, and it was a rendezvous for fishing boats and coasters.

As one looks downward now from the insignificant spot called Dunstan Landing, he sees a rather wide waterway extending in a perfectly straight course for more than half a mile to the railroad bridge. The Pine Point road location is by its side. This is "the New River," so called, and is an artificially constructed canal. Mr. James Frank Coolbroth, my good old-time friend, told me, when I said that it must have been a great undertaking to excavate this formerly deep and wide ship channel, that really it was not a formidable job. The Old River, meaning the Scarborough River, extended in a long, winding loop of several miles Northerly, Easterly and Southerly past the Manson Libby Hill, Skippers Point and Harmon's Landing. It made a troublesome course for vessels, and especially so for those carrying long masts. Across the Neck of this oxbow-like route a straight ditch was dug Southeasterly from the Landing through the marsh which had a tough, peat-like surface and soft subsoil, to a point near the present railroad. When this was done, wholly by hand labor, a dam was built across the Old River at the head of the ditch, and the tidal rush of the sea water backward and forward did the rest of the work thoroughly, and after a time made a fine channel.

The old story is that Dunstan, meaning the Landing and its vicinity, was in the early days and until after the Revolution quite as much of a business place as Falmouth Neck, by which name Portland was known after 1658 until it became a separate town in 1786. This tradition is probably correct, but requires explanation. Trade then consisted principally of exports of lumber and fish, and Falmouth had less of those articles and was more difficult of access from the back country, while Dunstan was an easy outlet for the immense product of the primeval pine forests in its rear, as well as of the abundant harvest from the fishing grounds off the Scarboro coast. But it must be remembered that the natural advantages of Old Falmouth had from the first made of it a conspicuous object for hostile attack. It was depopulated in 1676 and again in 1690, and almost completely destroyed by Mowatt's bombardment in

THE RIVERS AND THE OLD SEAPORT 53

1775. Little rebuilding was done there after the Mowatt devastation until the war was over. The eight years of the revolutionary contest was a period of harassment along the coast and especially upon the sea; Scarboro River and Dunstan were comparatively inconspicuous places and were less exposed to attack by British cruisers.

Before the war began it is said that a ship load of wood and supplies were contributed by Scarboro people and forwarded to

SCARBOROUGH RIVER BAR

Boston, at the time when commerce with it was forbidden by the Boston Port Bill, proclaimed by the English on account of the tea episode. Another cargo of lumber sent there was stated to have been sold to the British and used for making stalls for army horses in the Old South Church. The report of this alleged sale created a great scandal.

THE SITE OF THE OLD SHIPYARD—DUNSTAN LANDING

X

The Shipping and the Shipyard

X

THE SHIPPING AND THE SHIPYARD

MOST of the commerce in the early days was necessarily water borne. Good highways had not come into existence. The interior, until after the British capture of Quebec in 1759, was open to the constant risk of French attack. During the Revolution, British war ships were a continual menace along the coast. Even the fishermen and their boats were liable to capture. It was this danger that made the rebuilding of Portland too hazardous to be undertaken. Dunstan, being quite a distance up the Scarboro River, was so far removed from the sea that hostile naval vessels were not likely to attempt a raid, especially after the English had the rough lesson taught them at Machias. And so Dunstan had its opportunity.

There were, however, other places of shipment in the town. In the very early times locations giving convenient access to the rivers were established as public "Landings." The old Proprietors Records, which give the allotments of lands and the laying out of highways, show also the setting apart of places for common landings. These rights of approach giving connection with water routes were for public use like highways and were fully as important. Those still well known are Harmon's Landing, on the Scarboro River, near the Samuel Manson Libby Hill, and Seavey's Landing, near the mouth of the river on the Blue Point side. The Clay Pits Landing, three acres in extent, on the East side of the Nonsuch, for the convenience of Black Point and others, was laid out as appears by the proprietors record, Oct. 3, 1729. There were also water approaches at the Black Rock, at the old Scarborough River Landing adjacent, and at the Ferry Rock near Prouts Neck, and also on the Spurwink River and at other places. At these Landings were groups of houses, but by reason of its location

Dunstan and its seaport accommodations became for quite a long time the most prominent of all as a business locality.

The recovery from the demoralization of the Revolutionary War was slow. The National Confederation of States, with its worthless currency and general impotence, followed for six years. But the adoption of the Federal Constitution in 1789 gave general stability and sense of security. The land titles in Maine, which in the early days were in controversy and confusion, had been quieted by Massachusetts laws. There was, after the Revolution, a great inflow of immigrants to Maine. Portland, which by the first census in 1790 had a population of 2246, while Scarboro had 2235, began a great boom of development, having a population of some 7,000 in 1809, and Scarboro too in lesser fashion felt the impulse. Farming became profitable; lumbermen grew rich. Among other things my grandfather's tannery commenced operations. For many years the Dunstan Landing had been a port and a market place for the adjacent territory. It is still an open public landing.

In addition to its commercial business it was for many years noted for the building and launching of ships. There, just at the sharp bend of the river where the public shore right is conspicuous, was an excellent location for the launchings, and along the bank were established one, and probably more, shipyards. After business fell away it continued to be called "the shipyard." The Napoleonic wars, before and at the beginning of the nineteenth century, gave to the Americans who were neutral, a great opportunity. In the first half of that period they did a large part of the carrying trade of the world upon the ocean, and ships of all kinds were in demand. All along the Maine coast were ship owners and ship building. It was said that Maine built schooners by the mile and cut them off according to purchasers' requirements.

THE SHIPPING AND THE SHIPYARD 59

The young men quite generally went to sea. Dana's "Two Years Before the Mast" was typical of the experience of enterprising boys of the period. Mr. Coolbroth said there were frequently two ships upon the stocks at the Landing at the same time, and he thought that once within his remembrance there were four in process of construction together there. The launchings of the ships were events, when crowds gathered and schools were suspended. The last launching was about the year 1855.

My grandfather told of building ships quite far inland, and of hauling them with a line of ox teams on log frames to be put into the water at the Landing. Major Waterhouse on the Payne Road built a good-sized ship in his dooryard near the location of the old town house, and another was constructed as far away as the Flag Pond.

There were fishing vessels that sailed regularly on trips from the Dunstan Landing, as well as from other places. Grandfather owned a quarter part in a boat, of which one Coolbroth was skipper. This boat was lost in a great storm when, as he said, the reckless boatman thought he could make himself safe in the lee of Stratton's Islands instead of coming into port, with the result that the craft was wrecked and the captain and his boy were both drowned. From Blue Point and Black Point fishing vessels went on trips of several months to "the Banks," off Newfoundland. Other vessels fished along the Scarboro coast and elsewhere. There were flakes all around, where regular and occasional fishermen dried their stock of salt fish for winter consumption and for sale. A considerable part, like the mackerel, were shipped in barrels.

One Capt. Job Seavey, he said, was a happy-go-lucky skipper, but notoriously unreliable. A party from Buxton once took the precaution to send a messenger in advance to engage a fishing trip with him for the coming Thursday. Capt. Job readily assented, when his wife interfered and exclaimed, "Why, Joby, you know you have got to be away Thursday. Why do you tell the man such a story!" "Be still, woman," said Uncle Job, "I just didn't want to hurt his feelings." Uncle Job lived at Seavey's Landing. This, with Jones' Creek in rear of Pine Point and the Scarborough River Landing were probably the fishing settlements.

After the dyke was put in, just above the Eastern Railroad Bridge in 1877, to shut out the overflowing tides from the marshes, all the streams there shrunk to small proportion of their former size, and the once busy landing lost all resemblance to a port. As one now sees the quiet spot, mention of it as a busy mart provokes a smile. Nevertheless, at the time when about ninety-seven per cent of Americans lived outside of cities, this place was decidedly prominent and had well-known residents. Col. Thomas Westbrook and Benjamin Blackman as well as Richard King and others of note did business there. It is said that the first big masts that went abroad for English ships were sent from Dunstan Landing. Pepy's Diary tells how dependent the English Navy was upon American pines for its masts. Probably those of Nelson's ships grew in Maine. Uncle Jacob Milliken, who died at Dunstan in 1884 at the age of one hundred, said he had seen both sides of the Landing road from Dunstan Corner to the river, a distance of half a mile, almost completely covered with piles of lumber waiting for shipment, and that the Landing with its men and teams was an extremely busy place. The lumber piles could not have been continuous, for there were dwelling houses on both sides of the road.

Consideration of the geography of the place affords an explanation of its prominence. Scarboro, by reason of its division by rivers and marshes, was commonly referred to as being composed of three sections, "Black Point," "Dunstan" and "Over the River," each quite isolated from the others. It was a long journey by land around the barrier of the tide water limits and over Scottow's Hill to Black Point and Prouts Neck. It was also quite a long and circuitous route to reach Blue Point, a locality somewhat by itself, by way of the old road along the course of the Stuart Brook. But row-boats and sail-boats were abundant and communication by water was easy. It was, in the earlier times, much more convenient to go to Portland or to Boston and other places by water than by land. Dunstan acquired superiority largely because, although its port facilities were farther inland than any of the others in town, it had far easier connection with the country in the rear by the highways which centered there. Some of the other places in the town excelled in fishing, and perhaps were equal if not superior in their local shipping, but Dunstan had the advantage in general business connection with markets abroad.

The sea-shore, now so popular, had little of attraction. The Over the River part of the town, as the district above the Nonsuch River was called, was settled considerably later than the rest and was more especially agricultural, being occupied by well-to-do farmers with extensive timber lands.

When peace came, after the Revolution, Portland with its splendid harbor quickly advanced in commerce. Willis says, that though ships came and went from that port, there was not in 1787 a ship owned in that town, but in 1793 there were eighty, and after that the increase in tonnage was sudden and immense. The little local shipping places like Dunstan Landing were soon overshadowed for good and all, though the ship building there went on, together with something of local commerce for a good many years.

GOVERNOR WILLIAM KING

XI

The King Family and Resident People

XI

THE KING FAMILY AND RESIDENT PEOPLE

THE bend in the river at the Landing gave, for the adjacent country, water communication with the ocean from the time when the Algers made their settlement. The shipping of masts for the royal English navy was a large and very profitable business and was conducted by Col. Thomas Westbrook and others. The agents of the British government went through the forests, placing the royal mark on trees. The giant Norway pines were straight and lone, and it may have been this fact that suggested the excavation of the New River Canal. Richard King, prior to the Revolution, had a saw-mill location on the Western River, below its junction with the Foxwell Brook. He changed his residence to Dunstan Landing and became the prominent merchant of the place. He is said to have done the largest lumber business in Maine. He also had a store there and carried on extensive general business.

The King family had many distinguished members. Richard King himself came from Watertown, Mass., about 1744. His ancestry is uncertain. He built at the

KING ELM—SITE OF RICHARD KING HOUSE—BIRTHPLACE OF WILLIAM KING

Landing a fine two-story colonial house with addition containing a big kitchen, located near what is still called the King elm tree on the Easterly side of the road. The house had many windows with small panes of glass. Within was a wide hall with broad winding stairway, having the walls ornamented with oil paintings of landscapes and figures. The house was afterward long oc-

BURIAL MOUND OF RICHARD KING FAMILY, SCARBORO

cupied by Capt. Solomon Harford and after him by Hiram A. H. Googins. The old historic mansion became dilapidated with age, and instead of having it repaired, it was, somewhere about the sixties, torn down and a new modern house erected in its place, which stands substantially on the same spot. On the broad stairway in the main house was preserved the scar made

BOULDER ON RICHARD KING BURIAL MOUND, SCARBORO

by a rioter's axe at the time of its invasion by the so-called King mob just prior to the Revolution. King died before the war was actually commenced, but he had urgently counseled moderation and thereby aroused considerable feeling against him among the more impetuous. A rough crowd of men, said to have marched from Gorham, came to his house one night and threatened him with personal violence. He was always a thoroughly patriotic man, but had been in the King's service as commissary in the expedition against Annapolis Royal in 1745, and was much impressed with the power of England and her Navy; so the story was spread abroad that he was a Tory. There was also envious jealousy of King on account of his large landed possessions. He was accustomed to take conveyance of land in payment of store bills, and as land values were nominal, he was said to have acquired about three thousand acres, though this statement is perhaps an exaggeration. He, however, owned a geat part of the salt marshes and from them obtained a substantial revenue by selling the standing grass annually. He also had large holdings of fine timber land above Dunstan, and owned the Easterly end of Pine Point, and as was said, "Everything that joined him." Richard King was in fact a worthy and public-spirited, patriotic citizen. He died land poor. The oldest son, Rufus, was sent to Harvard, but the youngest, William, who was a boy of seven when his father died in 1775, had but little school education.

The Scarboro Kings became known at home and abroad. Three of the sons of Richard, born in Scarboro, were especially prominent. Rufus, after graduating from Harvard, went to Newburyport, Mass., and afterward to New York. He was a member of the Convention that framed the U. S. Constitution and was influential in its adoption. For a long time he was United States Senator from New York, was minister to England, and in 1816 ran as Federalist candidate for President of the United States against Monroe.

William King, the youngest son, was President of the convention that adopted the Constitution of Maine and became the first Governor of the State. He was a Democrat and strongly opposed the support of churches by taxation. He won much favor by his "King Betterment Law," designed to protect the holdings of squatter settlers.

Cyrus King graduated from Columbia College, N. Y., and settled in the practice of law in Saco. He served two terms in Congress from the Maine first district.

Another son, Richard, Jr., lived on Scottow Hill and was chiefly known for his peculiarities, and was often referred to as "Old Dick King." The King burial mound, near the Broad Turn road above Dunstan, marked by a large granite boulder, contains the remains of Richard King and members of his family. The lot was fenced by Edward King of New York and given to the Maine Historical Society, which now holds the title.

Governor William King is interred in Bath.

It is rather curious that this little hamlet should have produced a candidate for President of the United States (Rufus King); a member of the U. S. Constitutional Convention (Rufus King); the first Governor of Maine (William King); a member of Congress (Cyrus King); a Judge of the Court of Sessions (Robert Southgate); a long time Register of the Probate Court (Horatio Southgate); and nearby, Squire Joshua Fabyan, Rev-

"LEANTO" OF RICHARD KING MANSION—DUNSTAN LANDING

olutionary Tax Commissioner for Maine, a Court Judge and member of the first Board of Overseers of Bowdoin College. Edward Milliken, Esquire, also was a Court Justice. Joseph Willard, President of Harvard College, whose mother Eunice married Parson Richard Elvins, was raised in Dunstan. Dr. Alvan Bacon and his two sons were prominent physicians. The ministers, Parson Benjamin Chadwick and Parson Nathan Tilton, were Harvard graduates. The two Doctor Sewalls, the Emersons, Donnells, Jewetts and others were likewise people of reputation.

KING FAMILY AND RESIDENT PEOPLE 71

OTHER PEOPLE AND PLACES

On the Southwesterly side of the Landing road, about half way to the corner, are some elms in the field. These mark the location of the first residence of old Judge Robert Southgate. He came from Liecester, Mass., in 1771, and was a physician and also a Judge of the Court of Common Sessions. Dr. Southgate, as he was most commonly called, was a man of high character and influence. He married Mary, daughter of Richard King, and afterwards acquired a large part of the King lands. Dr. Southgate was a man of hardy frame and was an expert well builder. Several old wells in the neighborhood, still in perfect repair, are said to have had the stone work placed by him. He told my grandfather that he intended to do labor sufficient to get into a good perspiration every day. His daughter Eliza wrote a book published by the Scribners, containing a series of sketches of "A Girl's Life Eighty Years Ago," telling of the extensive hospitality of the Dunstan Landing home and of festivities in the fine families in Scarboro and Portland. After the turnpike road was opened about 1805, largely through the initiative of Dr. Southgate, he built the big brick house on the Northwest side of the Portland road, occupied later by his son, Judge Horatio Southgate, Register of the Probate Court, and now owned by Col. Fred N. Dow. His son, Horatio, was a Bishop of the Episcopal Church. Old Dr. Southgate died in 1833.

On the Southwesterly side of the Landing road, also across a ravine, which is the outlet of a spring of remarkably pure, cool water, is a wide, level space now partly covered with trees. This, as Uncle Jacob Milliken pointed out, was the drill ground for the Scarboro militia in Revolutionary times. Just in the rear, Westerly of this piece of table land, was a timber lot covered with monster pines of the primeval forest. These trees stood until the Southgate real estate was sold to Ezra Carter, Jr., and Seth Scamman in 1864, when the lot was cleared. Many of these trees were four feet and more in diameter. Some were said to have furnished three thousand feet of lumber.

Many Scarboro men were in the Revolutionary army. At the siege of Boston, though in the winter season, it is said that every man and boy that could carry a gun was there, and when Washington called for new recruits the reply was that only women with their scissors were left in the homes, as the men and muskets had already gone. It is, as has been said, a tradition that the Scarboro contingent were in the regiment that led the procession that entered Boston after the evacuation by the British. Scarboro men took part in the ill-fated expedition against Bagaduce or Castine, and were much mortified at the unlucky result.

XII

Old Dunstan Corner

XII

OLD DUNSTAN CORNER

DUNSTAN CORNER, now commonly known as Dunstan Village, and being the present location of West Scarboro Post Office, is about half a mile Northwesterly from the Landing. It is the region without any definite bounds, adjacent to the present corner made by the entrance and crossing of the Broad Turn road at the Portland-Boston Highway. The Broad Turn road, called earlier the North West Mast road, was the main route of communication between the interior and the place of shipment at the Landing. The Old road, so called, to Stroudwater Bridge and Portland now diverges from the newer Turnpike road at a little distance to the Northeast. The new Dunstan school-house stands near the junction of the Old road and the Turnpike road. This Broad Turn road was probably of more importance to the place than the ancient Portland route. It connects with the Portland and Boston road just at the Northeast side of the old Second Parish meeting-house lot, and evidently got its name from its wide entrance, communicating with both the Portland highway and the road to the Landing. This old road was one of the first to be widened and straightened by the town and was given a width of three rods. It extends to Scarboro Corner, as the locality adjacent to Buxton is called, and at that place makes connection with Bar Mills and Over the River section. Just beyond "the plains," so called, it crosses the Nonsuch River at the place called Rocky Hill, where its course on the Southeasterly side takes it over almost bare ledges. That on the other side is called the Fogg Hill. The two hills at the sides of the river crossing there are notably bad and steep. This Broad Turn road led through a region of magnificent pine forests. The part over the plains for a distance Southeasterly from Rocky Hill, now almost destitute of residences, had a good many houses, some large, but mostly small. The local name was "Plum Street." A considerable portion of the dwellers there in the forties got the Ohio fever and went West.

Westerly of the crossing of the roads at Dunstan, where the soldiers' monument now stands, was the location of the first built Church of the Second Parish. This parish was, according to the then existing law, incorporated by the Massachusetts General Court in 1758. It was a territorial parish, that is to say, a district, including lands and the people resident. All the property within its boundaries was subject to taxation for the support of church and minister. In that way it was distinguished from a so-called poll parish composed of individuals only. Before 1758 the whole town had been a single parish, and the minister was engaged by vote of the town meeting. After the establishment of the Second Parish with definite bounds, the First, or Black Point, parish included the remainder of the town.

The Dunstan meeting-house lot included an area of an acre or more and made a large village green. Church and parish were always spoken of as matters of first importance. My grandfather had some recollection of this Church building as an imposing structure of two stories with a steeple. Inside there were galleries and a high pulpit, having a sounding board in rear. The pulpit was high so that the preacher could readily be heard by the people both in the galleries and on the floor below.

The old village, before the four-rod county highway was laid out in 1803, connecting with the new turnpike, and before the limits of the Broad Turn road were established, must have been somewhat scattered and irregular. The old Boston and Portland road (called sometimes in its Southerly direction the Dover Road, because Boston was so far away) had originally many crooks and turns and it made at Dunstan a considerable sweep

OLD DUNSTAN CORNER

Southerly towards the Landing to avoid the meeting-house lot, which bounded upon it. This is shown by the fact that the present highway four rods wide goes across that lot, and a small strip of it which touched the Northwest side of the old roadway was cut off and is now within the limits of the Dunscroft Hotel field. A part of the Moulton House Hotel also encroaches upon the Parish land. All of the houses now standing were built afterwards or were adjusted to the present highway lines.

Dunstan Landing at the close of the Revolutionary War in 1783, had pretty nearly reached the heights of its importance. When merchant vessels began voyages upon the ocean and stage coaches came on, the small river landing places became of little consequence. The development of the United States after the Federal government became established was phenomenal, and Maine in its growth was among the foremost. Traveling by land took the place of slow water communication. In 1786, when Falmouth Neck became a separate town by name of Portland, it had about 2000 inhabitants. By the year 1800, its population numbered more than 5000. In 1775 a post office was established in Falmouth and mails sent by horseback conveyance. In 1781 a mail wagon, presumably two-wheeled, took its slow way to Portsmouth. The next year three mails per week were sent through to Boston, being allowed four days for the journey. In 1880 Vaughan's bridge was opened, and in 1802 the sending of a daily mail began reaching Boston in the brief space of twenty-seven hours.

The carrying of mails suggested passenger service. Then the demand for highway improvement began. Roads were, as has been said, widened and straightened. Then over Vaughan's bridge, across the Scarboro turnpike along the new highway, straight across the meeting-house lot went the coaches at reckless speed. Leaving Portland at two in the morning, if the roads were in good condition, they would be in Boston at ten o'clock at night.

In the early times travel by land had been wholly on foot or horseback. Prior to the Revolution there was an occasional "one-hoss shay" with two wheels and body supported by leather thoroughbraces. Considerably after 1800, with the development of roads, four-wheeled wagons made their appearance. That of my grandfather was among the first. After the decline of water traffic, lumber was still shipped from the Landing. The shipyard still kept up its operations and it was a haven for boats and small vessels, but its commercial importance was past. The fact that Dr. Robert Southgate removed from his place on the Landing road and built the conspicuous brick house on the Northwest side of the new Turnpike road is an example of the change. It was a period of substantial prosperity. Many square two-story houses were erected. "The Corner" became a local rendezvous and stopping place for the stage coaches and a distributing point. The Scarboro Post Office was established there in 1795. It had several well patronized taverns. There were also stores and blacksmith shops. It had also "Squires" who had law trials at their houses, and doctors, ministers, a town school of academic grade and private schools. It was indeed a prominent little village until some time after the steam railroads came in the forties; and when the lure of the Western prairies called many of its people away it became stranded and a place of quiet homes.

XIII

Old Times in the Vicinity

OLD PARSON LANCASTER PARSONAGE, BLACK POINT

XIII
OLD TIMES IN THE VICINITY

AM indebted to my Grandfather and also to uncle Jacob Milliken who died in 1884 at the age of 101 and also to James Frank Coolbroth, son of Rufus and Grace Reynolds (Runnels) Coolbroth, for general mention of people and residences in the locality. James Frank was an esteemed resident of Scarboro and resided near Prouts Neck. He was born in 1828 and lived to be the oldest man in the town. In his younger days he was a cooper and for some years went regularly to the West Indies winters. The shooks for barrels were shipped from the vicinity and coopers went to set up the barrels. Uncle Frank, as he was called, told me a good deal about affairs in this locality. His father, Rufus, was a ship carpenter and lived just across the Portland road from the old Dunstan school-house which stood upon higher ground called the Hill, and the school-house lot adjoined Southwesterly the Parson Benjamin Chadwick homestead. In his younger days uncle Rufus worked in the shipyard at the Landing. Aunt Gracy, his wife, was an uncommonly bright and active woman, with opinions of her own, and was a ready assistant to her neighbors in times of sickness. She came when a girl from her home above Rocky Hill to help at a shipyard boarding house and there met uncle Rufus. It was good form for girls from well-to-do families to go out as "help." The Coolbroths, by the way, were probably of Scottish descent and the name Americanized from the Scotch Galbraith. Uncle Rufus was my boyhood friend and was an erect, gentlemanly and very intelligent man and had a bit of Scotch accent. James Frank, the son, remembered well affairs of the first half of the century, after the highway lines had become established as at present.

There were, he said, several blacksmith shops in the place. William and Harris Burnham had a shop at the corner of the

Broad Turn and Portland roads, on premises now owned by the St. Louis Home for Boys. Their specialty was shipyard work. Samuel and William Warren had a blacksmith shop on the Southeasterly side of the Portland road, afterwards the home of John S. Moulton who was a meat dealer. The Warrens did most of the ox and horse shoeing and were also general traders in cattle, some of which they took in droves to Brighton, Mass. Amos Hight, who lived on the place now the Dunscroft Hotel, had his shop across the road where William H. Graffam's store now stands. He specialized in edged tools and other implements. His broad-axes for hewing timber, of which my grandfather had one, as well as his other tools had quite a reputation.

There were several stores at the Corner, changing from time to time. These were general stores, where all kinds of goods were sold and exchanged for produce. Simon Milliken had a store adjoining or enroaching upon the S. W. side of the meeting-house lot in front of his tavern. Thomas Richards had a variety store on the Northwesterly side of the road where the Knight store and West Scarboro Post Office is now located. He did a large business and after his decease his widow, Phebe Carter, married Freedom Milliken, who had been a clerk there, and they continued the business for a long time. Henry R. Williams had a store on the Southeasterly side near his tavern where the big spreading elm stands. Johnny Beaudin, a Frenchman, perhaps a descendant of a French family brought to Scarboro at the time of the Acadia deportation, had a little store with a hall called Temperance Hall above it on a lot adjoining and N. E. of the Dunstan cemetery lot. There were other stores of a more or less transitory nature. After the meeting-house was removed from its old lot Judge Horatio Southgate claimed to own the land, though it was used as a village green. No one seemed to know any basis for his claim and he did not force it.

The old Dunstan Cemetery for a long time had no apparent owner or care. It was used commonly for burial purposes and some families took possession of parts of it for individual lots. It was the general custom of land owners to have private burial places on their own premises. There was apparently no other common church-yard in the vicinity of the old meeting-house. The town afterward purchased adjoining land and took possession of the whole as a town cemetery. The remains of those interred in private lots were quite generally transferred to this cemetery.

There were fences along all the roads. It was customary for some people to let their cattle "run in the road" and use it for pasturage. In recent years the road fences have been removed. Drovers of cattle from the Northern counties passed through the place, usually on Mondays, taking their herds to the general cattle market held weekly at Brighton, Mass.

When the French Canadians were deported from Acadia in 1755 they were transported by the English government in detachments to the American Colonies. Those sent to Massachusetts were apportioned by the General Court to the several towns, and four by the name of Boudrix came to Scarboro. It is not known whether or not they remained, though there were afterwards several having French names in the town. Johnny Beaudin, who has been referred to as having a little store at Dunstan, was a Frenchman and John Burghy who lived at the cross roads between Oak Hill and Coalkiln was also said to be a Frenchman. From him the Baptist meeting-house, called the "Buggy" meeting-house, received its name as it was built adjacent to Burghy's place of residence. Both of them were good, quiet citizens.

The deportation from Acadia which is commonly called barbarous, was in fact considered a matter of military necessity and was quite carefully done. These "Neutrals," as they called themselves, were on territory in Nova Scotia taken by the English and they were unchangeably French in their sympathies. It was then a time of life and death contest between the French and English for the possession of this country, and such a hostile colony was a menace to New England. The proposition was to distribute them among the colonies, expecting they would assimilate. No families were separated unless by mishap and the plan would have worked out well except for the invincible religious and racial tenacity of the Acadians. The Longfellow poem "Evangeline" was chiefly imaginary and a poetic romance.

There were quite a number of negro families in the town, mostly descendants of the "servants" or slaves of the earlier days. The enumeration of inhabitants in 1760 showed eleven slaves in the town. Captain Timothy Prout had a black servant by the name of Caesar who married the colored servant, Hagar, of Madam Elizabeth Deering. They and their children were baptized members of the First Parish Church. Slavery was recognized until abolished by the Massachusetts Bill of Rights in 1783. They generally died off or moved away and no new comers of the race appeared in their places. A few were in the Coalkiln neighborhood until about the time of the Civil War. An old colored man, named Caesar, was an occasional caller at my grandfather's place. Little Joseph Fabyan Carter, after gazing at him, once remarked, "Your face is proper dirty and you must wash that black off." Caesar was called apt and witty and when he accosted one Capt. Payne by saying, "Good morning, sar, what am the news," and the Captain answered, "Great news, Caesar, the devil is dead," replied, "Not surprising, sar, I hear he been in *pain* a good while."

XIV

Taverns and Stage Coaches

Relay Stage Coach Horses

XIV

TAVERNS AND STAGE COACHES

IT CAN safely be said that the orderly development of Maine was more than a century behind that of Massachusetts and the other colonies. It was the first to be sought for and the last to be regularly settled. By reason of the contest of rival claimants no certain title to land was obtainable until the William and Mary charter united it with Massachusetts in 1691. The efforts of France to obtain possession, and her persistent incitement of Indian hostilities and raids, did not cease until the cession of French territory in America to England at the end of the seven years war in 1763. The English Colonial policy of King George the third, in the years immediately following that war, aroused resentment which caused rebellion, and the war of the Revolution began about ten years after the French contest closed. The eight years period of that war was a time of danger and distress. After the coming of peace the opportunity for safe and convenient settlement in Maine became apparent, and immediately there came a great wave of immigration. In the early times, while the French were exploring the interior, the English settlements were confined almost entirely to the sea-shore and the vicinity of the larger rivers. When the war was over many of the Revolutionary soldiers came to Maine, and Massachusetts made township grants of land. Farms, lumber mills, ship building, fisheries and other industries were opened up. The middle West had then hardly been explored. Of the far West little was known until after the time of the Lewis and Clarke expedition in 1805. The eager development of Maine created a demand for highways and better transportation by land. The old irregular bridle paths and winding courses gave place to improved roads for carriages. Portland early became a center for various lines of stage coaches. The war of 1812 caused interruption of sea routes and promoted travel by land. With the increase of passengers there came a demand for better accommodations of the traveling public and this requirement was met by the numerous taverns.

Dunstan was well supplied with taverns. John Donnell kept the Donnell Tavern, Northwesterly of and in the rear of the Second Parish Meeting-House lot. This was perhaps the principal hostelry and was for years a stopping place for stage coaches. It was a fine old two-story house and stood, it was said, for more than a hundred years. Mr. Donnell's daughter, Almira, married Dr. Stephen Sewall, son of old Dr. Stephen Sewall, and they occupied the mansion until the second Dr. Stephen's decease after the time of the Civil War when it was sold and a new dwelling erected upon the spot.

Simon Milliken, the store keeper hereinbefore mentioned, put an upper story on his house adjoining the meeting-house lot and had a fine establishment called the Scarboro House. This has been enlarged and with additions is the present hostelry known as the Moulton House.

Henry R. Williams, the same who had a store, kept also a tavern, being the building lately occupied by Bartlett Pillsbury with the large spreading elm tree in front. This was called the Elm House and was quite a local resort. Williams was a notably eccentric and contrary man.

The Millikens had a tavern at their place toward Saco beside the Stuart Brook. This was on the Southeasterly side of the main road and was commonly called Mulberry's tavern, and had stables on the Northwesterly side of the road opposite the tavern with accommodation for many horses and oxen.

The era of stage coaches developed with the improvement of the highways. It was about 1818 before through lines were in operation and they then continued until steam railroads were built subsequent to 1840. For a long time there were two

TAVERNS AND STAGE COACHES

through stage lines and two coaches went West and two East each day between Portland, then a rapidly growing town, and Boston. These through coaches were drawn by four horses and in bad traveling by six. The driver on approaching the village would blow his horn and crack his whip, and the galloping horses would come into the tavern yard in fine style. Once a week the mail coach brought the Scarboro mail. John Donnell was the first postmaster that Mr. Coolbroth remembered, though Eliphalet Smith was appointed when the office was established in 1795. After Donnell, Amos Hight had the office for a long time. The mail was sorted and left on a table in Mr. Hight's front hall and people generally looked it over and selected their own letters.

The building of the turnpike road made a considerable change, although some of the stage coaches and a considerable part of the general travel followed the old route rather than to pay the tolls. Many boys and foot passengers avoided the gate so that there was a beaten path through the bushes behind the toll house. There was a gate and a toll keeper's house at the top of the turnpike hill just beyond and Northeasterly of the Dr. Southgate house. Mr. Abram Milliken was for many years the man in charge of the gate and lived in the keeper's house and was also the town clerk. His son, John Alger Milliken, was later town clerk for a long time. The turnpike was built of gravel drawn by ox teams from the gravel pit near the Old Dunstan school-house, which until recently stood by the Old Orchard trolley terminal, and it was always kept in excellent repair. After the P. S. & P. railroad was built the through stage coaches were discontinued, but a passenger coach and a freight express ran from Portland to Saco until after the Civil War. After shipbuilding declined and through coaches ceased their journeys the busy days of village and taverns were soon things of the past.

All of the taverns and stores sold "spirits" quite as a matter of course, the established price being three cents a glass and the glass was of a size to hold a gill. A spoonful of molasses usually went with the toddy. At the shipyard a ration of West India or New England rum was regularly served at eleven o'clock. The old men always insisted that actual drunkenness was almost unknown, though there were some who drank too much and wasted their money in frequent glasses of the attractive beverage. There was, to be sure, much mirth when once the good parson could not mount his horse after a funeral. There never was a drinking saloon in Dunstan.

When the Washingtonian temperance reform developed, meetings were held and lectures given and sentiment became so strong that stores and taverns left off selling before there was a prohibitory law. The keeper of the Elm House for a while insisted upon keeping his bar open. The story was that a lot of men gathered one night and called him out and gave him a ride on a rail, whereupon he, too, unwillingly quit the business. The old gentleman, my grandfather, approved of the temperance movement, but when the enthusiastic advocates came to him and others with a paper for signature, stating that the signers were reformed drunkards and pledged themselves to abstain from their evil habits, he resented it, saying that he had always been practically a teetotaler.

In recalling the use of liquors by our ancestors we should consider the customs of the times. The possession of alcoholic beverages in some form was considered a part of the equipment of every well regulated household. When the minister made his pastoral calls a glass of "spirits" was the common token of courtesy, and the neglect to offer it was a discourteous omission. No general gathering was considered properly provided for without the usual stimulant. A hotel landlord or storekeeper who did not have the popular beverage in stock

TAVERNS AND STAGE COACHES

would have been an object of derision. Yet there were even then some who tended their bars unwillingly, thus showing that they observed the evil effects of strong drink; and the temperance reform had prompt reception. In the very early times, however, such an idea had no existence. The first liquor indictment found in this locality was that against John Winter of Spurwink. But in his case the complaint was not for selling liquor, but for charging too high a price for his aqua vitae or brandy, contrary to the common law provision against undue profits in the necessaries of life. The prohibitory law was a result of the temperance movement and not the cause of it.

OLD DONNELL TAVERN—DUNSTAN

XV

Over the River District

XV

OVER THE RIVER DISTRICT

THE town of Scarboro by conformation of its territory is divided into three quite distinct sections, namely, (1) Old Black Point; (2) the West side, including Dunstan and Blue Point; and (3) Over the River, including Coalkiln Corner, now called North Scarboro. The various streams that flow in serpentine courses through the wide expanse of the marshes separate Black Point on the East side, which was the earliest and most prominent settlement, from the Dunstan and Blue Point localities on the Westerly side. Before the turnpike and the railroads were built it was a roundabout and quite lengthy journey by land from one of these sections to the other. The common use of boats, however, made the difficulty less marked than it otherwise would have been. After the second settlement, so called, in 1702, Massachusetts laws were in effect and there was more of order and stability in regard to real estate titles, and when the more immediate danger from French and Indian hostilities diminished, the lands in the upper part of the town began to be taken up, and this newer part was referred to by a name of its own. The Over the River district was so called because it lies mostly upon the Northwesterly side of the Nonsuch River. Prior to 1720 there probably was not a white man's house North of Oak Hill or Scottow's Hill. Scarboro is rather level near the sea-coast but is quite elevated and hilly in the interior. On the high land, called Beech Ridge, one gets a particularly high outlook.

The winding Nonsuch River, which has its rise in North Saco, flows for a considerable distance from West to East and then makes a long detour Southward and enters the Scarboro River just below the Clay Pits Landing near Prouts Neck. Its entire length of some thirty miles after it crosses the Saco lines is within the old limits of Scarboro. It is said that one can go but little way North, South or East inside of the town boundaries without crossing the Nonsuch. The name of Nonsuch (often improperly spelled Nonesuch) is generally supposed to have been given by reason of its eccentric course, which in general outline is compared to a horseshoe. It is, however, claimed that the name originated from the neighborhood where the

NONSUCH RIVER MARSHES

river has its source. That region along the Southeasterly side of the river towards Scarboro Corner was, it is said, called in the old days Nonsuch from the immense size of the pine trees which grew there. Whether the river was in fact named from the locality or the locality from the river is quite uncertain.

Across the Saco line where the river has its beginning, on the farm formerly of Horace Sawyer, and also farther along, it takes early the inflow of quite a number of streams. Especially in the upper part, its flow is through broad and fertile intervale lands between steep hills on either side. Toward its mouth we find the name again in the Nonsuch Farm. It gathers so great a volume of water in times of freshet that it is impatient of bridges, as the town still knows to its cost. Before the timber was cut off and before New England farming was made unprofitable by the competition of the fertile West, this Over the River District was the most substantial and well-to-do portion of the town. It was the place of lumbermen and large, productive farms. In the choice of Selectmen one of them has by long established custom usually been apportioned to each of the three sections.

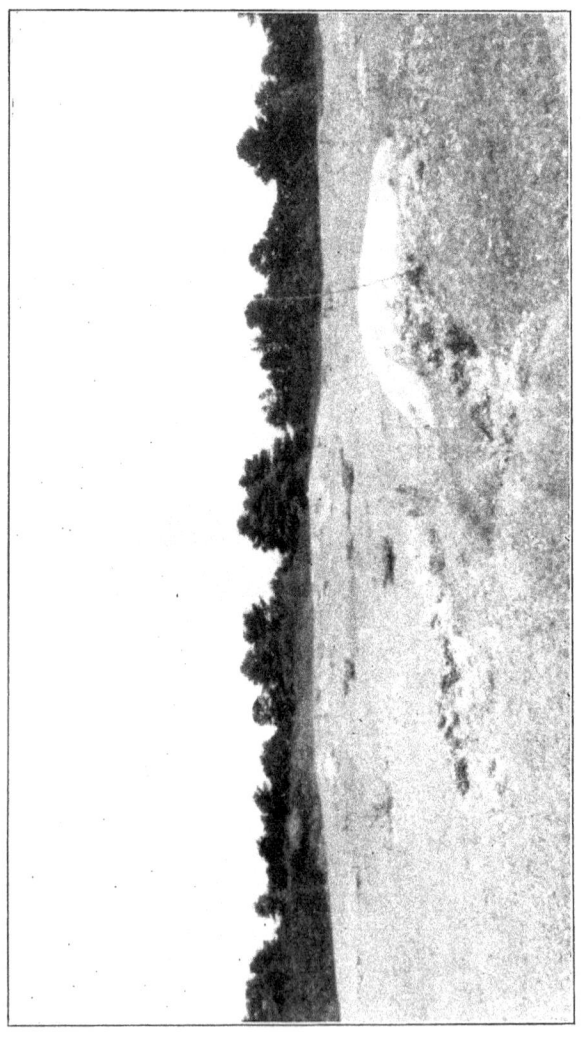

Indian Camping Ground—Winnock's Neck

XVI

Charles Pine and the Pioneer Settlers

XVI

CHARLES PINE AND THE PIONEER SETTLERS

N the Southwesterly side of the Broad Turn road was the later home of Charles Pine. This is what is known as the Carter neighborhood. That was his place of residence after the interior of the town was opened up. He was buried in the family burial lot on the premises as appears by his traditional grave-stone with no legible name. Pine's house site and grave are just Southwesterly of the road and Southeasterly of where it crosses the Nonsuch at Rocky Hill, being the place marked "D. Carter," in from the road in the 1873 Atlas of Scarboro. One of Pine's daughters, Sarah, married Benjamin Carter and another daughter, Grace, married John Reynolds. The granddaughter, Grace Reynolds, married Daniel Moulton, known as Captain Daniel. Charles Pine was one of the noted men of the second settlement. It is hardly open to question that he was the Pine who is mentioned as one of the defenders of the fort on Prouts Neck in August, 1703. The defense of this fort by eight men is one of the notable events and is mentioned in Parkman's history of the Half Century of Conflict. It has been questioned whether there could have been such a fort at so early a date. Willis, however, mentions settlers at Spurwink in 1697, and it is most probable that some of the first settlers would come back, even though temporarily, to their former possessions where they and their fathers had lived nearly sixty years prior to 1690. The tradition is too well established to be seriously questioned. The dubious peace of Ryswick between England and France, was made in 1697, but hostilities did not cease and began again openly with Queen Anne's War in 1702 and continued until the Peace of Utrecht in 1713. It is recorded that twenty-two were killed or captured in Baubasin's sudden attack upon Spurwink in 1703, and that one John Wallis escaped to Black Point carrying his

little son upon his back. The historical mention of the fort was probably made on account of its remarkable defence.

The residence of Charles Pine on Pine Point is marked on the map in Southgate's history. Pine and Richard Hunniwell are named as noted Indian fighters in many persistent traditions. A tradition is pretty certainly founded upon fact. No other Pine is mentioned. He was a noted hunter and the hero

GRAVE OF CHARLES PINE, INDIAN FIGHTER AND HUNTER, NEAR ROCK HILL, OVER THE RIVER DISTRICT

of daring adventures. An allotment of land was made to him as a non-resident in 1720, though quite certainly he was not a land holder of the first settlement when the rental system of land there prevailed. There is no account of his origin, though the old folk stories said that he came from London and received yearly remittances from abroad sufficient for his support. The origin of his son-in-law John Reynolds also is not traced.

CHARLES PINE AND PIONEER SETTLERS 103

It was said in the ancient tales that upper Scarboro furnished no inconsiderable part of the masts for England's royal navy. In the Colony times the King's officers went through the forests and marked the conspicuously tall, straight pines with what was called "The Broad R," indicating that by royal privilege they belonged to his majesty and must not be cut by any individual. The letter R, standing for Rex, the King, when carefully cut into the bark of a tree made a conspicuous mark that could not be effaced. Some of those trees stood until recent times. A hill in the region is still called Mast Hill. British ships were largely dependent upon America for masts and prices were high. It is not unlikely that some of the mighty pines that went down the Broad Turn road and out from Dunstan Landing had their part in the naval battles of Drake and Nelson.

Rev. Peter Libby, the old land surveyor, clock repairer and preacher, once told me that Captain Daniel Moulton, who married Grace Reynolds, granddaughter of Charles Pine, and lived southeast of Rocky Hill, owned more than a mile of Nonsuch meadows, and used to gather a crew of men sufficient to mow all the grass upon one side of the river in single swaths and returning, cut the other side in like manner. The captain was one of the town's conspicuous men and was a member of the Committee of Correspondence and Safety in the Revolution. The stumps from the big trees were used considerably for fences and in that locality there may still be found, after the lapse of a century and a half, portions of ancient stump fences.

The lumbermen used their axes with great skill for many purposes, from the felling of a tree to the sharpening of a lead pencil, and often took an axe along as a man would carry a cane. Rev. Peter told me that the rather gruff Captain Daniel one day called, axe in hand, upon his son Charles, who married Olive, a sister of Squire Joshua Fabyan, and was a blacksmith and lived on the Southwest side of the Broad Turn, up the hill Northwest from the Nonsuch. Charles with pride took his father into the cellar to sample a barrel of West India rum which he had just obtained and "horsed up" for winter use. The old Captain took a draft and then remarked, "That is good rum, Charles, and I'll show you a good way to dispose of it so that it won't do you any harm." Whereupon with a blow of the axe he smashed the head of the cask and let out the contents upon the cellar floor.

On all the streams in this region of big timber and fertile land there were saw-mills. In most places there was not sufficient water to do business except at a time of spring freshets and in the rainy periods when the mill ponds would fill up, as it required much water to turn the wasteful water wheels. This explains why there were so many mill sites on small streams.

The people then and in the later times raised the greater part of their food supplies upon their farms, and had good stocks of cattle and lived in well-to-do and substantial comfort. The promissory note of a farmer unsecured by mortgage was considered about the strongest kind of investment. He could not then put the place "into his wife's name."

Uncle Aaron McKenney who lived at the Saco Heath neighborhood across the Saco line and died in 1880 at the age of 102, told me a curious story about the departure of the wolves. The keeping of sheep was necessary on account of having the wool for clothing, but the sheep had to be gathered into folds at night by reason of the danger from wolves, which were numerous and troublesome. Swine were quite generally kept for protection on islands and that is the reason why so many were named Hog Island. One winter there were organized parties for frequent wolf hunts. Along in March, the old gentleman said, there came a considerable fall of light snow and one night there was an amazing gathering and commotion among the wolves. The air seemed filled with their howlings as they ran about, and the people within their houses were alarmed by the strange occurrence. When morning came, he said, there were wolf tracks in every direction. In many places they had run in circles and the prints in the new snow showed where they had sat down in groups as if in consultation. Every wolf, however, was gone, and he said, so far as he knew, there has been no wolf in the vicinity since that night. This seemed to me at the time merely as one of the folk lore wonder tales, but in books of natural history mention is made of other occasions where wolves in similar fashion have left their old haunts in a body and returned no more.

Uncle Aaron said that when he went to live on his place at the Heath, it was mostly unbroken forest around, and that he rived out and shaved shingles by hand and carried them upon his shoulders to Dunstan, and sold them there.

The Broad Turn road, or Western Mast road, was for a long time a much used thoroughfare. There were houses and homes along both sides, as is still attested by the frequent cellars that are reminders of the dwellings once standing there. For a mile or more Southeasterly of the Charles Pine or Carter neighborhood and through the level plains, where now scarcely a building appears, it was so thickly populated that it, as it has been said, became known as Plum Street, a name still applied to it by the older inhabitants. This is a tract of poor land with small houses, now gone, and people not well-to-do.

The passing years have brought about altered conditions in the town. Hotels and summer visitors have rejuvenated Black Point and the sea-shore. The electric cars have to some extent again awakened Oak Hill and Dunstan, but farms are not profitable and the Over the River district has not maintained its former high estate. The younger people quite generally seek homes elsewhere.

XVII

Random Grandfather Tales

XVII

RANDOM GRANDFATHER TALES

UST below the Eastern Railroad the Dunstan or Scarboro river turns abruptly Northeasterly, then back again Southwesterly, making a long loop. The lower part of this cape-like reach is called Greenleaf's Point. There Richard Hunniwell had his adventure with the Indian whom he killed with his scythe. The upper part where the river takes another bend seaward bears the name of Jane's Point, commonly called "Jean's Point." At this place up the southerly river bank is a ravine having near its head a spring of remarkably pure water called Jane's Spring. On the side of this sheltered ravine, facing Southeasterly, my grandfather said was the cabin of the squaw, Uphannum or Jane. She was one of the grantors in the Indian deed to the Algers of their Dunstan tract. She survived her family, and even through the Indian hostilities quietly occupied her lonely habitation until she died there at the age of more than a hundred years. It is said that this feminine trader, after having sold her interest as the white men assumed, three times, was pacified by receiving an annual tribute. Her fire-place with its blackened hearth-stone was pointed out there until about 1890 when a man who was building a cottage at Prouts Neck, now the Lyons Tea Room, purchased the old hearth-stone and dismantled the fire-place. The stones were built into the new structure. Soon these stones became obscured and all knowledge of their identity was lost. This destructive desire for antiquities seems truly like sacrilege.

Not less tragic is the story of the eagle's nest in the same locality. From this the well-known Eagle's Nest picnic grove received its name. There, in an ancient pine, a pair of white-headed eagles had their nest almost from time immemorial. They were regarded with a sort of superstitious reverence and long made their home in the same tree undisturbed. I myself have seen them circling high up in long, graceful curves, their white heads and necks almost glistening in the sun. Some years ago an ambitious sportsman crept up to the home tree and shot the male bird and the female disappeared. This performance was little less than wanton bird murder.

In the rocky pasture on the Easterly slope of Blue Point Hill towards Seavey's landing, the old inhabitants used to point out with bated breath "the bloody hearth-stone." This was and probably still is, if it may be located, a piece of rose-streaked quartz standing out in the ledge. The tradition is that this rock was stained with the blood of Mary Deering who was murdered by her husband there, and that the stains can never be effaced. She was a daughter of Charles Pine, and her husband, William Deering, seems to have been a worthy man. From the accounts it would manifestly appear that he had become insane. The case caused tremendous excitement far and near. Deering was tried and sentenced to be hanged, but the sentence was not executed and what end he made is one of the mysteries.

The old gentleman had clear recollection of the war of 1812 and the wars of "Old Bony," as he called Napoleon. He had great admiration for "Bony," who he thought gave the tyrannical kings and aristocratic lords a well-deserved upsetting. He spoke of no great interest being taken in the war in this part of the country. The Britishers were too busy watching out for Bony to do much here. They, however, made the business of the fishermen very hazardous, as they captured any Yankee craft that they found afloat. The danger to coasting vessels was so great that it stimulated the travel by land and the establishment of the stage coach lines. Several times there were alarms about anticipated attacks upon Portland, and a company of young men was raised in the vicinity. He remembered them as they marched along the road to Portland where they encamped on the hill, now Fort Allen Park. They were there, he thought, several times and then returned home.

He took part in an interesting episode that he related with much satisfaction. It seems that during the embargo which preceded the war, there had been a great deal of smuggling and the Spurwink River was a place where vessels often unloaded their illicit cargoes. This continued even while the war was in progress. There was in this town a government officer whose duty it was to intercept the smugglers. One afternoon, my grandfather had notice to join a posse to make a raid upon a smuggling outfit. They were unarmed but marched off boldly. The small company arrived at the tavern on Oak Hill considerably after dark. There they stopped to refresh themselves with crackers and rum, and the landlord informed them that there was a lot of smugglers down by the shore all armed with guns and "bagonets." At this the commander lost heart and declared it was no use to go any farther. Grandfather protested, and the officer told him he might have command and go ahead if he saw fit. Most of the others were willing to follow him, so he took the lead and they resumed their march. After going some distance they came to low ground where there was a thicket of black alders. This was what he had been looking for, and he ordered the men to whip out their jackknives and each cut an alder and take a piece about the length of an ordinary musket. Then with their wooden sticks upon their shoulders they advanced until they heard the trampling of men and teams. Grandfather waited until the law-breakers came near and then in a loud voice ordered his men to halt and make ready, and commanded the smugglers to surrender or take the consequences. In the darkness the alder sticks looked like real guns and the smugglers instead of surrendering fled, leaving teams and everything behind them. There was a great lot of broadcloths and valuables, which the posse took charge of and turned over to the government officials. The affair created a good deal of amusement and grandfather received secret warnings that reprisal would be made upon him. He told 'em that he wouldn't go abroad a minute sooner nor stay at home a minute later on account of the occurrence, and nothing came of it.

He remembered well the sea fight between the Yankee privateer, Enterprise, and the British war brig, Boxer, on the Maine coast in 1813. The next day after the battle he was in Portland. He visited the wharves where the two ships lay at anchor side by side and went with other visitors on board the Boxer. The ship, he said, was terribly battered and the decks were covered with splinters and blood from stem to stern. The sailors of the two ships were fraternizing and talking about the fight. He heard an Englishman say to a Yankee, "You had too many guns for us," and the Yankee replied, "Count them up, we had no more than you, but we fired three broadsides to your two, and our aim was true while your shots went wild." They told him that Blythe, the English captain, had his flag nailed to the mast head (which is an historical fact), and when the Captain was dead and the ship hopelessly unmanageable, they could not get at the flag but gave token of surrender by leaving the guns and running back and forth from one end of the ship to the other.

He was an interested participant in the trainings and was an officer in the militia. The military organizations and these trainings of the militia were for years matters of general interest. After the Revolution it was determined that the country must thereafter be prepared and kept prepared for defence, and all the young men were put through a course of drill. In the years of peace after the contest closed, the lessons of the Revolution in that regard were mostly forgotten, and the war of 1812 found the American people with their old military leaders gone and in a most discreditable condition of helplessness. After that war it was again said that never again should such conditions occur, and a system of universal military training was adopted. Every young man was enrolled in the militia, and each year was obliged to attend the musters "armed and equipped as the law directs" when the companies were brought together for general reviews on training day. There were crack companies and "string bean" squads. The training day was one of the annual events, and it resulted in producing a great crop of captains, majors and other military titles. My grandfather regarded the militia gatherings as noteworthy occasions, but before the outbreak of the Civil War the whole system had become obsolete and disused.

After the war of the rebellion there was again a general revival of the spirit of preparedness. I myself at Bowdoin College was put through a pretty vigorous course of training under a regular army officer for a year, but the idea became prevalent that modern civilization had got beyond the barbarism of settling disputes by armed conflict, and the World War again found the country forgetful of the lessons of the past.

The visit of Lafayette to this country in 1824 was an occasion of national interest and enthusiasm. My grandfather remembered it well. He thought that no individual ever received such a reception and such a welcome. Lafayette came from Boston to Portland in an open carriage drawn by four horses and with a retinue of attendants on horseback, stopping at all the various towns and villages. All along the road were decorated arches bearing the motto, "Welcome Lafayette." At Dunstan there was a fine arch and a reception with a great gathering of adults and school children cheering and shouting "Welcome." The Marquis was then an old man but genial and alert. His common greeting to a man was to ask if he were married, and if he said yes, the Frenchman would reply, "O happy man." If the answer was no, the response would be, "O you lucky dog."

Grandfather did not consider the modern improvements and growth to be hardly compensation for the stately dignity of the good old times. He loved to recall the days when the town meetings were arenas of debate and consumed two whole days, the first being regularly at the Black Point meeting-house in the First Parish and the second, the adjournment, at the Second Parish meeting-house at Dunstan and later in the Tilton meeting-house up the Broad Turn Road. Then as generations came and went such worthies as the Kings, the Southgates, the Stuarts, the Marrs, the Libbys, Jewetts and other townsmen of equal merit—not of course contemporaries, but whose memories live in the traditions of the town—took part, and the moderator called out "Order, gentlemen" as he polled the house; and there on one sensational day, William Moulton, from Over the River, won his title of The Duke of Scarboro, conferred upon him by one Graffam who cried out—"Make him Duke and let him go it alone," because he seemed to be too influential at the meeting. For a long time the town meetings were regularly held in the meeting-houses.

Prior to the fifties a town house was built, after a contest and compromise, and located near the geographical center of the town at the crossing of the Payne and Vinegar roads. Everybody then was supposed to be interested in town affairs and the meetings were productive of much oratory. In 1883 the new town house now standing was erected at Oak Hill as the result of heated controversy and political trading which revived the old jealousies of the two parishes. The establishment of the trolley line has made the location accessible and convenient and allayed the rather bitter feeling.

The old gentleman knew by tradition of the ancient routes of communication. First such travel abroad as there was, confined itself to boats and small vessels. This made Richmond Island, Stratton's Islands, the Isle of Shoals and other ports to be places of importance for stopping and trading. It was quite an advance when bridle paths were established for horseback riders. A trail left Portland, always prominent by reason of its harbor, and passing around the upper part of Fore River went down through Cape Elizabeth to the Spurwink River where there was a ferry about a mile from its mouth named for Ambrose Boden, thence the route was over the Black Point plains —being the name of the level ground along the shore—to the Ferry Rock Southeast of Libby's River near Prouts Neck, at the Western point of what is now the Country Club grounds. There a ferry man had a boat to take the traveller with his horse across the Scarboro River to the Easterly end of Pine Point; thence he followed the long beach Southwesterly, fording Little River, a shallow stream, now dammed up by the Boston and Maine Railroad extension, and its outflow turned into Scarboro River, past Old Orchard to the Saco Ferry where another ferry boat took him across. From that point he went on by blazed path to York, Portsmouth and Boston. There was an early trail called the King's Highway along the shore from Pine Point to Old Orchard. This was the general course, but it is idle to attempt to give, except at the water crossings, more than an outline of the route, for the riders, who were only occasional, varied their paths and made cut offs according to season and individual fancy. Willis, in his history of Portland, gives an interesting account of the so-called roads or trails which were not, of course, established by any legal authority. It should be noted that there were two places called Pine Point, one on the Northeast side of the Scarboro river near the Black Rocks and the other on the Southwest side as now known.

XVIII

The Indian Wars and Garrison Houses

XVIII

THE INDIAN WARS AND GARRISON HOUSES.

HE early history of Scarboro has many traditions relating to the Indians and the Indian Wars. The seashore and the marshes were resorts of multitudes of wild fowl. Fish abounded in the rivers, streams and along the coast. The clams especially furnished food both in Summer and Winter. At Winnock's or Plummer's Neck and at other places are great shell heaps, showing that it was for unnumbered years a Winter home of the natives. They lived in groups or tribes which were supposed to be descended from common ancestors. They did not recognize authority derived by descent, which was reckoned from the mother. The chiefs and sachems were leaders selected generally for their physical prowess and mental capacity, and were deposed and changed at any time. This fact was not well understood by Europeans and was a cause of frequent mistakes, as it was commonly assumed that a chief might himself make agreements binding upon his tribe. The men were warriors, hunters and wigwam builders, while the women attended to domestic affairs, cultivated such crops as were planted and prepared the food. Marriage was not known, but they lived in pairs and were generally faithful to each other, but separated and made new family relations according to fancy.

They had no fixed places of abode. The tribe would go to one spot for planting and then to another for hunting or fishing and occupied sheltered camping grounds for Winter residence. The Indian's mind had no idea of individual ownership of land any more than of water or air. They had, however, regional locations upon which no one was allowed to intrude without permission. The white man's deed of conveyance had no meaning for them other than as a permit to share the occupation without objection.

At the first coming of the random settlers the Indians regarded them with rather cautious and suspicious friendship. They were pleased to barter their furs and products for the goods and wares of civilized people. Beads and trinkets were much desired, being far superior to their laboriously wrought wampum and personal ornaments. Fire-arms and iron tools soon took the place of bows and arrows and stone implements. The better class of whites knew that it was politic to keep on good terms with the aboriginal occupants, though there were quite often bad and drunken men who made trouble. On the whole there was for more than forty years, an era of good feeling between the races. When the harvests ripened the planters in Scarboro regularly made contributions to their Indian neighbors, either as a peace offering or as a tribute, and they bought and bartered for their furs and game. The Indians mixed freely with the settlers.

Some grandfather traditional stories illustrate this phase. A thriftless Indian hunter, he said, called upon a white man and told him he had left the carcass of a fine deer under a big elm tree in the nearby meadow and asked his friend to buy it at a bargain. The white man paid the price but was unable to find any deer. The next day the Indian drifted along and the white man demanded an explanation. The noble red man asked, "Did you find the meadow?" The answer was "Yes." The next inquiry was, "And didn't you find the elm tree?" The reply was, "Yes, easily." "And didn't you find the deer?" asked the hunter. "I sure did not," declared the white friend. "Well," said the Indian, "that was two truths and only one lie. That pretty good for Injun."

A settler hired an Indian for a shilling to kill a calf. The Indian promptly did so and turned to go. "But you haven't skinned the calf," said the settler. "That nother job and nother shilling," said the aborigine. The white man paid the additional shilling, the hide was neatly removed and again Mr. Indian made ready to leave. "The calf is not dressed nor finished," exclaimed the planter. "That nother job and nother shilling," replied the dusky workman, and the white man had to produce the third shilling in order to get his work completed.

The old traditions say that in addition to those who came to establish themselves as settlers there were temporary people that had come, some as fishermen and others as lumbermen, who built saw-mills and helped themselves to the limitless supply of wood and timber. A few were hunters and sportsmen. By 1675 there was in the three divisions of the town Black Point, Blue Point and Dunstan, a considerable population who had made clearings and were occupying them with their families. As early as 1641 there is mention made of a minister, indicating that there was a considerable population. After the authority and laws of Massachusetts were recognized in 1658 there was a marking of individual homesteads. There were in many cases close friendships, and many of the natives learned to speak English. The rougher class of white men, however, made trouble.

It is said that Squando, the Sachem and Medicine Man of the Saco tribe, was a friendly praying Indian. The story is told that at the critical period, when King Philip's emissaries were abroad, some drunken fellows at Saco Falls seeing an Indian squaw in a canoe with her baby, thought they would find out whether it was true that an Indian could swim naturally. They upset the canoe and the baby sank. The mother rescued her child but soon after it died. These victims of brutal folly proved to be Squando's wife and his only baby boy. As a result, the kindly chief became an enraged and bitter enemy. There was, about this time, a disturbance to the eastward where several Indians were killed upon slight provocation. Some of the Indians told their intimate friends that trouble was impending. The Boston authorities notified the Scarboro people of danger, and told them always to go to meeting armed, but except to fit up a few houses with loop-holes for garrisons nothing was done.

In the early autumn of 1675 the blow fell with the stealthy suddenness characteristic of Indian warfare. It does not seem to have been an organized attack. A roving, hostile band found Robert Nichols, an old man, with his wife in their house on the Easterly side of the Foxwell brook or Western River near the present old Blue Point road, and killed both of them and burned the house. The Dunstan settlers gathered about the Alger garrison and the Indians withdrew without making an attack there. The white people left their homes and concentrated at Black Point. A month later an attack was made upon the Alger garrison house at Dunstan, which was held by a few men. Andrew Alger was killed and Arthur Alger mortally wounded. The place seems then to have been wholly abandoned. There were several garrison houses in various occupied parts. These it is impossible to locate. Foxwell's garrison was probably near the Watts saw-mill, afterward the Richard King mill, near the present electric railroad. There was on Blue Point the Shelden's garrison and at Black Point and at other places quite a number. These were only log houses with loop-holes for firing from within. The principal place of defense was the Scottow's garrison, the old residence of Henry Joselyn at Garrison Cove on the Pine Point side of Prouts Neck. The next year an attack was made upon this Scottow garrison by Mogg Heigon or Hegone, Whittier's Mogg Megone. This was a very intelligent and capable Indian chief. His principal residence was the "Arrowpoint" cape, West of Saco River, and he spoke English freely. He had been induced to sign a deed to William Phillips by which, "for a sum of money" he surrendered all of the present town of Kennebunk, the heritage of his people. The fort, or garrison house, was surrendered and all of the people left the place. The Indians did not remain and a part of the people soon returned to their homes.

GARRISON COVE—PROUTS NECK, 1870

The next year, May, 1677, Mogg made another attack with a large force upon the fort. The siege continued three days. In a direct frontal charge, a thing quite unusual for Indians to undertake, Mogg was killed. This ended the attack and Mogg's followers buried him and his slain companions nearby and retreated. Within a few days, a company of Massachusetts soldiers, under command of Capt. Benjamin Swett and Lieut.

James Richardson, arrived for aggressive war, with headquarters at the Prouts Neck fort.

Unknown to them, a force of some five hundred Indians gathered, apparently to avenge the killing of the great chief. A month after the death of Mogg, June, 1677, the English force with some friendly Indians were skilfully decoyed from the fortification and led on into an ambush at Moor's brook near the present Black Point school-house.

This was one of the most bloody of Indian battles. Swett and Richardson were killed with forty of the English, being nearly half of the force. The survivors succeeded in regaining the shelter of the fort.

In 1678 a dubious peace with the Indians was made and the Black Point settlement was largely resumed. In 1681 the great fortification, Scottow's fort, was constructed. This was on the ridge in the field Westerly of the Atlantic House. It was a large stockade of wooden palisades set upon ridges of earth. Part of one of the bastions or flankers is still plainly apparent in the edge of the woods. This fortification afforded protection and Black Point again became quite prosperous.

In the meantime Count Frontenac had become Governor of Canada, and he promoted continued hostility with the Indians. His methods were crafty. When the Indians were disposed to be peaceable he would send bands from Canada to make raids and keep hostilities alive. In 1688 William and Mary came to the English throne and Louis XIV declared war. In 1690 a great expedition was organized and a large force swept over Maine. Fort Loyal in Falmouth was taken. Defence seemed hopeless and Scarboro was wholly abandoned and continued vacant of white men for a dozen years.

Queen Anne's war came on in 1702. Evidently people kept coming irregularly to attractive Scarboro, for Parkman who explored the old French records tells of the successful defence of a garrison house in Scarboro in 1703 against an attack by a large force of French and Indians. This was the garrison on the present West Point House location on Prout's Neck, where eight resolute sharpshooters baffled an army. Then followed what Parkman calls the "Half Century of Conflict." Those of the Second settlement, so-called, had nothing of governmental kind more than a so-called "combination," which meant an irregular assembly for acqaintance and mutual action, until after the peace of Utrecht between England and France in 1713. After that the town record book was brought back from Boston, where it was carried in 1690, and in 1720 town government resumed. Indian raids were all the time threatened, and it was a period of almost romantic and wholly venturesome conditions.

In 1723 a general attack was made. Two Larrabees were killed at Black Point and the garrison house of Roger Dearing on the Hasty place or Nonsuch farm at Oak Hill, was captured. The destruction of the French outpost of Father Rale at Norridgewock in 1724 broke the force of the French attacks, though Nathaniel Dresser was killed by the savages as late as 1747. There were no really safe situations, and the place was in constant apprehension until the capture of Quebec by Wolfe in 1759 ended French dominion in America.

From 1675 to 1759 there were three Indian wars, or more accurately it may be said, there were three periods of active conflict with intervals of distrustful quiet. The old folk tales of Pine and Hunniwell and lesser participants are without number. There were rude garrison houses in all the occupied sections of the town. The exact location of but few are known. Vaughan's garrison, later occupied by Seth Storer, and the Roger Dearing garrison, near the Portland and Saco road, recently owned by S. D. Plummer, the Little Red House at the partings of the road Southeast of the Oak Hill Railroad Station, the David Libby garrison on Scottow's Hill and Shelden's Garrison on Blue Point had considerable of permanency. In other locations only the names remain.

It is said that there were thirty or forty garrison houses in Scarboro. Tradition has it that the Little Red House garrison still stands upon the spot where Richard Hunniwell's family were massacred by the Indians.

The French and Indian wars developed unspeakable ferocity. The French offered rewards for English scalps and the English paid for Indian scalps. For the natives it was a war of extermination. They could not make peace, though evidently they often desired to do so. Any effort for pacification was followed by murderous raids by the so-called "Christian Indians" from Canada with disguised French contingent. This gave to the Indians a reputation for utter treachery. The French had no consideration for their red allies. The result to the Indians was almost entire extermination. They were driven from pillar to post and could do little for their own support. Far more perished from famine, disease and exposure than from English bullets. Nearly all of the pitiful survivors at the end of the conflict went to the Indian colony near Quebec, where some of their descendants may still be found. On the other side the losses of the English were tremendous. In the first three years war more than half of the settlements in New England were destroyed. Maine as a frontier State was most of all exposed, and prosperity in Scarboro was long made impossible by the clouds of danger and warlike uncertainty.

XIX

Black Point and Prouts Neck

XIX

BLACK POINT AND PROUTS NECK

THE beginnings of Scarboro in a legal way date from the patent of November 1, 1631 given by the Council of New England, otherwise called the Council of Plymouth, to Captain Thomas Cammock of fifteen hundred acres of land on the East side of the Black Point River. This patent is found in York Registry of Deeds, Book 2, Page 87.

It conveyed regular title and was confirmed by so-called livery of seizen with turf and twig in 1633, this being recorded in the same Registry, Book 2, Page 85. The tract in general terms comprised the territory Southeasterly from a line beginning at the Black Rocks now owned by Dr. Willis B. Moulton, on the Black Point, Owascoag or Scarborough River and extending Easterly to the junction of the Western branch of the Spurwink with the main river and bounded on the other sides by the Spurwink, the Bay of Saco and the aforesaid Black Point River. The boundaries were pretty definite, considering the very slight knowledge of the place possessed by the parties at the time.

There was then in existence in New England the little Pilgrim settlement at Plymouth, possession of which had been taken at random and without permission in 1620, also the beginning of occupation by the Puritan Colony of Massachusetts Bay at Naumkeag or Salem under their concession of 1628, also perhaps some remnant of the Richard Vines fishing station at Winter Harbor or Biddeford Pool granted February 12, 1630. George Cleeve and Richard Tucker with some attendants had fully established themselves the previous year, without written title, on the Easterly side of the Spurwink River, from which occupation they were ousted by Trelawney in 1632. Black Point therefore ranks among the first, if it was not actually the very first, except Pemaquid, of the regularly established settlements in this province of Maine.

At that time there was commencing what was almost a competitive rush for possessions in America. Fishing and trade here had been found to be valuable. We cannot now comprehend the extent of the fisheries. Thy were declared by an early writer to be worth more than the gold and silver mines of Mexico. The breaking up of the schools of migratory fish with seines, the wholesale methods of fishing, and the obstructions in the rivers have destroyed and frightened away these denizens of the deep almost as the game and wild animals have been forced to disappear on the land. Even fish have an instinct which causes them to abandon places found to be unsafe. Temporary locations, therefore, for business purposes were being taken up all along the coast. The natives were eagerly laying aside their bows and arrows and stone implements and with no knowledge of values, were bartering their hunting products for the white man's wares. No places, however, were then occupied by Englishmen except such as were readily accessible by ships.

The parts which afterwards became Scarborough were (1) Stratton's Islands; (2) The Cammock Patent of Black Point mentioned above, including the Neck; (3) Blue Point, and (4) Dunstan. The Over the River District was a wilderness. These occupations were independent of each other. The Stratton's Islands (Stratton and Bluff) were the earliest in occupation, having been taken possession of by John Stratton of Shotley, Suffolk County, England, some time prior to 1630. He had there a trading station for dealing in supplies required by the numerous fishing vessels from abroad and for carrying on fur and other trade with the Indians. He sold the islands to Capt. Thomas Cammock in 1640 and went to Cape Porpoise.

BLACK POINT AND PROUTS NECK

The Cammock Patent with its fifteen hundred acres was commonly called Black Point. Blue Point (Blew Point) was a plantation, so-called, occupied without authority or boundaries, and was apparenty reckoned as including the territory between the present Old Orchard and Saco line and the Scarborough River, and reaching back approximately from the ocean Northwesterly to the Foxwell's (Cascade) Brook or lower Western River.

The Council of Plymouth gave to Thomas Lewis and Richard Bonython in 1636 a territorial concession extending four miles Easterly from the Saco River along the shore frontage and extending Northwesterly eight miles into the interior. This comprised present Old Orchard and Saco bounding upon the present town line of Scarboro. Richard Foxwell and Henry Watts, two of the Saco settlers, with others formed an independent community on the Southwesterly side of what they called the Blew Point and what we call the Scarboro River.

Foxwell's Brook which unites with the Stuart Brook to form the Dunstan River still bears his name; and the Henry Watts saw-mill was easterly from the point where the electric railway crosses the stream. The early comers there were styled planters; widow Eleanor Bailey, one of the number, being a large owner and holding in her own name and right.

The Dunstan community was established about 1651 by the brothers Andrew and Arthur Alger who came from Dunster, England, and apparently were, for a time, with John Stratton upon his islands. The Algers, desiring something as a basis of title, obtained from the squaw, Jane Uphannum and her mother, they being daughter and widow of a Sagamore unknown except as mentioned in this transaction, a deed of something more than a thousand acres called the Alger tract of Dunstan.

These four communities, Stratton's Islands, Black Point, Blue Point with Dunstan and the lands running back eight miles into the country were set apart by agreement with Massachusetts in 1658, twenty-one years after the Black Point grant, as a separate town by the name of Scarborough. The assertion of authority by the Massachusetts Bay Colony is commonly called usurpation, but her charter in its literal wording plainly included this part of Maine, and its date was about six years prior to that of Gorges' grant.

Black Point, meaning the Cammock patent, was established as an aristocracy with a feudal proprietor and rent paying tenantry, but the rest seems to have been occupied under what we would call squatter's title with something of citizen's communal control called combinations. A recital of the land titles of Black Point, including Prouts Neck, hereinafter stated gives a pretty good idea of that locality and its history.

When Henry Jocelyn came into possession in 1643 he found the Black Point title disputed. The Cromwellian revolution in England against the divine and absolute rights claimed by the then King, Charles I—had begun with the meeting of the Long Parliament in 1640. The parliamentary party asserted that under Magna Charta the King could not legally give away territories without the consent of the people's parliament. King Charles had then, by virtue of his sole prerogative, given to Sir Ferdinando Gorges in 1639 a royal patent of the Palatinate of Maine with its lands and with full governmental powers, ignoring all prior conveyances. The Lygonia patent of 1630, being prior in date to the patents of Cammock and Gorges, was in 1643 brought to the attention of the parliament and its committee decided that, being the earliest charter, it took precedence. The province of Lygonia was revived and George Cleeve was appointed Deputy President or Governor. Civil war began in England and the Gorges, Cammock royalists here

BLACK POINT AND PROUTS NECK

were unwilling to accept the parliamentary decision. The province of Massachusetts Bay, upon its part, came forward with the assertion that a survey of its Northern boundary line showed that a part of Maine, including Black Point, was within its chartered limits, Massachusetts asserted its authority, which became quite generally recognized in Maine, and it was by virtue of this claim that Scarborough was established as a town in 1658 with fixed boundaries. Henry Jocelyn became a prominent public character and his holding of Black Point and the Neck was retained by him. When the Protectorate of Cromwell ended in England and Charles II was restored in 1660 the parliamentary decision was reversed and the royal Gorges titles were restored.

With this turmoil of titles the Black Point establishment of business and tenantry could not prosper. Jocelyn accumulated debts instead of profits, and July 16, 1666 mortgaged all of his feudal properties to Joshua Scottow, a merchant of Boston. July 16, 1666, he made full conveyance or livery of his holding, and the Black Point patent thus became the property of Joshua Scottow. The occupation of Jocelyn covered a period of about twenty-eight years.

The primary claim of English ownership began in 1606 when King James chartered a company authorized to make grants and promote English settlements in Northern America. This company was divided into two independent parts called the London Company and the Plymouth Company or Council for New England. The latter had jurisdiction over present Maine. In 1620, no successful settlement having been made, King James issued a new charter to the Plymouth Company. This patent is reckoned as the basis of the English land titles. In 1622 the Council of Plymouth voted a grant to John Mason and Sir Ferdinando Gorges of lands comprising substantially the provinces of Maine and New Hampshire. This action, it seems.

though voted was not consummated, but Mason and Gorges by virtue of it made an agreement for division by which the part Northerly of the river Piscataqua was to go in severalty to Gorges. In the eager effort to promote settlements and the lack of knowledge about the country, grants were made without much regularity. June 26, 1630, an allotment of territory forty miles square which included Black Point was made and named the Province of Lygonia. Occupation under this award was attempted but was not continued. Then November 3, 1631, the Council for New England made its said grant of Black Point, comprising fifteen hundred acres, to Capt. Thomas Cammock, nephew of the Earl of Warwick, who was President of the Company, stating that he, said Captain Cammock, had lived in New England for two years last past.

From this Cammock patent, thus traced from King James himself, the record title of Black Point including the Neck definitely begins. In all this there must be kept in mind the fact, long manifested here, of the distinction between the possession of the soil and the right of government. Under the ancient doctrine the King by divine right was owner of all the lands in his dominions and had also by the same divine right full authority to govern. The sovereign bestowed upon the Council for New England, as his agent, liberty to apportion lands, but did not give them or their grantees permission to make laws of their own. Cammock in his territory could rule as a feudal lord but could give only leases of the King's lands to his tenantry.

Thomas Cammock held the title twelve years and at his decease in 1643 the whole estate with its liberties and privileges passed by his combined deed and will to his wife Margaret Cammock for her life-time, with remainder to his well-beloved friend, Henry Jocelyn. The widow soon married Jocelyn who thus became owner in fee.

Henry Jocelyn retained an uncertain ownership for thirteen years when in 1668 he transferred the patent to Joshua Scottow, a merchant of Boston. The ownership was disputed and uncertain. The revival of the old Lygonia grant of 1630 had resulted in the appointment of George Cleeve as Governor, but Massachusetts retained her control of this part of Maine and her laws were quite generally recognized. The adherents of Gorges were rebellious and a law case was pending in England, brought by the heir of old Sir Ferdinando to regain the province. Decision of the King's Court gave it to young Ferdinando, the grandson and heir. Massachusetts then purchased the Gorges charter and province. Then came the revocation of her own charter in 1684 followed by the tyrannical rule of Andros in the King's name. The second English revolution came in 1688 when William and Mary were made King and Queen. In 1691 the New Province Charter was granted which united Maine with Massachusetts. Indian wars beginning in 1675 and intermittent French and Indian occupation from 1690 to the peace of 1759 added variety to existing conditions.

XX

The Prouts Neck Title

XX

THE PROUTS NECK TITLE

THE following abstract from the York records gives the chain of title there appearing from the beginning:
Book 2, Fol. 87. The Council for New England Nov. 1, 1631 by virtue of grant from King James to said Council dated Nov. 3, 1620 conveyed to Capt. Thomas Cammock in consideration "that he, said Capt. Thomas Cammock, has for two years last past lived in New England and there made improvements," and also payment of rental 12 pence for each 100 acres forever, a patent of 1,500 acres of land upon East side of a river known by name of the River of Blac. Poynt, with privileges and rights and with two Yslands called Strattons Ylands."

Book 2, Fol. 85. Livery of seizin of above to Thomas Cammock dated May 23, 1633.

Book 2, Fol. 85. Sir Ferdinando Gorges to Capt. Thomas Cammock. Gives grant anew and confirmation of the said premises and privileges, saying that he, said Ferdinando Gorges, is absolute Lord of said Province of Mayne in free and common soccage, Dated March 15, 1640.

Book 2, Fol. 84. Capt. Thomas Cammock to Henry Joselyn, Esq., deed and will, with consent of wife Margaret. Consid. 100 pounds sterling. All his lands at Black Poynt with goods, chattels and personal estate, reserving 500 acres adjoining River of Spurwink to bestow at his pleasure. Dated September 2, 1640.

Book 2, Fol. 6. Henry Jocelyn to Joshua Scottow of Boston, merchant, in consideration of 484 pounds sterling. Mortgage all the 1,500 acres named in grant with the two Yslands and 750 acres adjacent and all other property. Dated July 16, 1666.

Book 2, Fol. 98. Henry Jocelyn, Esq., to Joshua Scottow. Certificate of possession and seizin of all lands at Black Poynt given July 25, 1668, in lieu of the whole contained in the above mortgage of July 16, 1666. Transcribed from original July 6, 1671.

Indian hostilities began in 1675. The inhabitants were driven away but returned. Scottow built his stockade fort in 1681. The French with Indians captured and destroyed everything destructible in 1690 and the place was left vacant. Joshua Scottow died in Boston in 1698 leaving a will by which all his estate was given to his wife for her life-time. His sons-in-law, Maj. Thos. Savage and Capt. Samuel Checkley, were appointed executors of his will. Maj. Savage died and Samuel Checkley acted alone as Executor.

Book 21, Fol. 276. Samuel Checkley, Esq., Executor of the Will of Joshua Scottow, merchant, deceased, "by virtue of a license from his Majesties Court in Boston," after the decease of Mrs. Scottow, conveyed to Timothy Prout, merchant, the tract of land at Black Poynt 1,500 acres with all rights, liberties, etc. thereto appertaining. Dated April 1, 1728.

Timothy Prout took possession and occupied with his children. He made sales of parcels of land. His claims of overlordship and rental payments under his deed were ignored. He apparently assumed to live something like an English Squire with his lands and properties, including some black servants or slaves. He attempted to obtain by law an additional large tract of land, asserting that the Northwestern boundary line, which was given in his deed as extending from the forks of the Spurwink River to the nearest point on the Black Point River was the true line and therefore claimed a limit to a point above the Clay Pits Landing. This would have more than doubled his holding. He lost his contention in an expensive law suit. The surveyor's plans then made give the bounds of the old Cammock patent and his additional claim.

THE PROUTS NECK TITLE

When Captain Prout died, April 5, 1768, he left a complicated will distributing his estate among his heirs. The will was somewhat obscure and his debts were considerable and there was much litigation. The continuation of the title record may be found in the Cumberland County Registry of Deeds, which begins with the year 1760.

The Prouts appear to have been an excellent family of somewhat aristocratic tendencies, and inclined to believe that they could live upon the landed estate left them by the wealthy Captain Timothy. A partition of the lands was attempted after his decease but with unsatisfactory results. The daughter Mary married Capt. Alexander Kirkwood who had served in the English navy. He was a shrewd Scotchman. The settlement of the estate came into the hands of Judge Robert Southgate of Dunstan. The Kirkwoods acquired all of the Neck proper except the holding of Joseph Prout on the Easterly side. They built the two-story house, which had brick ends, fronting upon Garrison Cove, and which became the Libby Mansion and hotel. The peninsula was then called Kirkwood's Neck.

Alexander and Mary Kirkwood conveyed in 1783 to Timothy Prout Hicks, a grandson of the original Timothy, the Easterly end of the Neck, 61 acres, together with the Kirkwood homestead, 7 acres (Book 12, Page 181). Hicks in 1788 conveyed both parcels to Robert Libby (Book 16, Page 15). The Westerly end of the Neck, 51 acres, was deeded by Mary Kirkwood to Judge Southgate in 1801, it is said in payment for his legal services. In 1807 Southgate transferred the same Kirkwood 51 acres to Robert Libby and Thomas Libby, 3d (Book 72, Page 13). It thus continued until Capt. Thomas Libby, 3d, purchased of Robert Libby January 11, 1830 (Book 122, Page 4) the Hicks land on the Eastern side, the Kirkwood homestead on the Northwest side, and his interest in the Southgate tract, the so-called Westerly end 51 acres, together with all of Robert's interest in the Prouts Neck real estate and thus became sole proprietor. Thomas Libby once attempted unsuccessfully to exchange his Neck for the Capt. Joshua Moulton farm in the Over the River district.

The Atlantic House, Scarboro Beach premises, 140 acres, lying near to Moore's Brook, came into the hands of Capt. Samuel Checkley individually and was by him sold for 100 pounds to Capt. Timothy Prout, March 24, 1727. York Deeds, Book 12, Fol. 276.

Black Point, the original name, was sometimes applied to the whole locality even after the establishment of the town of Scarboro in 1658. For years it was the principal part. When the Indian wars had subsided and the town meetings were re-established in 1720 highways were laid out and the back country with its large timber interest was developed. The Dunstan section then became more prominent. Passage by land and stage coaches, following the period of the Revolutionary War, took the place of water ways and boats, and Black Point and the Neck as its port lost their pre-eminence. The upper part of the town with its fine farms and its timber lands became the most prosperous and well-to-do section. With the opening of the sea-shore for summer resort this has now again been changed, and old Black Point has again come into the larger prominence.

XXI

The Churches and Parishes

XXI

THE CHURCHES AND PARISHES

MY GRANDFATHER was an intensely religious man. He had the Puritan inheritance but without anything of Puritan aggressiveness or intolerance. I never knew him to argue or sermonize. With him it was enough to deal justly, to love mercy and to walk humbly, yet with his well-worn Bible for his guide, he had lived through the time when religious controversy was like the heat of battle.

At the time of the New England settlements the period of religious bigotry and intolerance had not relaxed. The Thirty Years War, which was a religious war of fanatic and murderous import in Europe, did not come to an end until 1648. There was no such thing as toleration anywhere except in Holland and Rhode Island. Massachusetts excluded all except Puritans; Maine was distinctly a place for Church of England Episcopalianism. In Canada, from the time of the Hundred Associates in 1628 no one was allowed to remain unless he was a Frenchman and a devout Roman Catholic.

It is a matter of common knowledge that the first settlement in Scarboro was royalist and aristocratic, as distinguished from the Puritan republicanism of the Massachusetts Bay Colony, and that such religious institutions as they desired were Episcopalian with the forms of the Church of England.

The grant to Gorges provided for having a bishop with English Church establishment at Gorgeana or York, and it was soon determined to place the feudal province of Maine at the headship of New England. This would surely have been done had it not been for the English revolution of 1640 and the establishment of the Puritan commonwealth with Oliver Cromwell as Lord Protector.

The Scarboro tradition refers to an early church building on the Cammock tract of Black Point. It was spoken of in 1671 as an object of superstitious fear by the Indians. This indicates that it had probably been in existence there for some time, even before the Massachusetts occupation in 1658. It had also a church-yard adjacent, in English fashion. This structure, it is most likely, was Episcopalian. A Puritan church would have kept a record. Churchman Jocelyn calls it "our church." The number of inhabitants at Black Point, Dunstan and Blue Point had become considerable, and while there were new arrivals under the Massachusetts by the royalists, so-called usurpation, there continued to be also people of the old quality and denomination. Scarboro in considerable part remained faithful to the Gorges title and the old regime. Mr. Coolbroth told me that the location of this church was upon the Wiggin Farm, now owned by the Prouts Neck Country Club and stood on a slight mound, still apparent, not far from the site of the old Wiggin house and Northwesterly from it and near the Scarboro River. He remembered that there were quite a number of gravestones in the old church-yard and that they were taken up and used as a part of the foundation of the Ethan Wiggin barn. This church was destroyed in the French and Indian attack of 1690.

Until after the submission to Massachusetts in 1658 there were no town or church records and we get little information except such as comes from tradition and occasional reference in Court records.

In the Trelawney Papers mention is made of Rev. Richard Gibson, Episcopalian, who came to the Spurwink settlement and Richmond Island about the time when Cammock got his patent of Prouts Neck in 1631. Mention is made of the payment of Church tythes in English fashion by the planters. Mr. Gibson and Mr. Jordan, both good churchmen, apparently officiated in a ministerial capacity in Spurwink, Casco and Black Point, now Scarboro. Rev. Robert Jordan came to Spurwink in 1640 and was a militant Episcopalian of the strictest sort. He remained until the abandonment in 1690. Rev. John Thorpe was complained of in 1659 for preaching unsound doctrine which might have meant Puritan or Episcopalian theology, and Christopher Collins and Sarah Mills were prosecuted for being Quakers and refusing to pay the minister his "stypend." Rev. Benjamin Blackman, son-in-law of Scottow, was settled by the town as a minister in 1680. This was in accord with Massachusetts laws. Blackman was a Harvard graduate and a moderate Puritan. In 1686 Rev. George Burroughs, a devout and good man, came and was the last minister in the town during the first settlement. He went to Salem at the abandonment of the town and became a victim of the witchcraft delusion there in 1692.

The second settlement is regarded as dating from 1702. It plainly was no organized occupation. Yet there were people then at Cape Elizabeth. In 1703 there was a block house on Prouts Neck. The tradition of the attack upon this garrison occupied by Pine, Larrabee and the Libbys is too persistent to be disregarded, and it is quoted by Francis Parkman from the Quebec records.

One of the first things attended to by the town when again established was to provide for religious services, and in 1720 Rev. Hugh Campbell, a Scotchman, was by vote regularly engaged as minister. That there was no meeting-house appears from the fact that services were held at the house of Roger Dearing at Oak Hill, Samuel Libby at Black Point and Col. Thomas Westbrook at Dunstan.

In 1728, when Norridgewock had been captured, and the Indian wars had mostly subsided, so that there was a substantial permanent population, Rev. William Tompson, class of 1762 Harvard, was ordained and began a ministry which lasted thirty-one years. Upon the coming of Mr. Tompson the First

Parish Congregational Church was organized, which still exists. The town built in 1731 the first meeting-house, 40 feet in length by 35 feet in width, being a two-story building with galleries and located at the Northwest corner of the Black Point cemetery.

This first meeting-house of the Black Point church was used until 1799 when the upper part of the town having become developed, a new place of worship was erected on Oak Hill on the Portland road near the Gorham road and not far from the

OLD BLACK POINT (FIRST PARISH) MEETING-HOUSE

present town house. This was occupied until about 1850 and then a new house was built on the N. E. side of the Black Point road adjoining the Boston & Maine Railroad location. This is now made over into a residence by George M. Oliver. After that came the present neat church on the other side of the road, still in use.

THE CHURCHES AND PARISHES 149

Rev. Thomas Pierce, Harvard 1759, a Presbyterian, followed Mr. Tompson. He was ordained in 1762 and died in 1775. After him came Rev. Thomas Lancaster, Harvard 1764, a steadfast orthodox. He remained until his death in 1831. Father Lancaster was greatly beloved. He was the clergyman who married my grandfather and Sally Fabyan.

From about 1720 meetings were held at Dunstan which was then increasing in business and in importance. Mr. Tompson for a while resided at Blue Point and until the coming of Richard Elvins preached alternately at Black Point and Dunstan in private houses. About 1735 a meeting-house was built at Dunstan by the town on the village green where the soldiers' monument now stands. In 1744 a separate church was organized there and Rev. Richard Elvins was ordained as pastor.

I am largely indebted to my grandfather and Mr. Coolbroth for some details of church history at Dunstan. The first meeting-house was always spoken of as an imposing structure two stories in height with steeple and with galleries and high pulpit within. There is a rude sketch of it on the Milliken division plan of Dunstan in the Cumberland Registry of Deeds, Vol. 100, Page 571. The meeting-house lot was about an acre in extent and was spoken of as the common. The reason for the high pulpit was to give the minister a position where he could readily address the congregation on the first floor and in the galleries at the same time. The wooden pews were square with hinges attached to the seats so that they could be raised when the occupants stood up for the singing. With seats all around it was literally a family pew where the parents could keep a watchful eye upon the children during the long sermons. Sometimes the seats would fall down, making a noise, to the great delight of small boys. There were the deacons' seats in front of the pulpit and long slender rods in stock with which the deacons could touch and awaken any chance sleeper. Until iron stoves were invented there was no heat even in Winter in the churches. Some took charcoal foot stoves or heated stones to church. This was, however, frowned upon as unnecessary luxury.

Mr. Elvins was an ardent and devoted minister. He had become converted in the great religious revival of George Whitefield, who was a coadjutor of the English Wesleys, and came to America on a preaching tour. Mr. Whitefield, upon invitation of Mr. Elvins, preached in the Dunstan Church when he visited Maine in 1 7 4 5. Parson Elvins was a faithful administrator as well as preacher. His congregation and pastoral field took in Old Orchard, a part of Saco, Blue Point, Beech Ridge and the Over the River district. People went a long way to church. Many took their dinners and made a day of it. There were regularly preaching services in the forenoon and in the afternoon and an evening prayer meeting at early candle light. The Sunday meeting was not only a religious occasion but likewise a general convention. There were no newspapers and few books and the church service was the intellectual recreation of the people. At noon time they would assemble in

SOLDIERS' MONUMENT—LOCATION OF OLD SECOND PARISH CHURCH

THE CHURCHES AND PARISHES   151

groups and, after proper discussion of the minister's sermon, would rehearse the news of the day, the neighborhood gossip and the old stories and traditions. Those who did not go to church felt that they were left behind in the way of general information.

Mr. Elvins regularly made the circuit of his extensive parish mounted on his old mare with saddle bags, traversing the winding and tortuous highways and bridle paths.

By special act of the Massachusetts General Court in 1758, Scarboro was, as has been said, divided into two parishes, the First and the Second. The Second Parish embraced the territory West of the Owascoag—Scarboro River, including Beech Ridge and Over the River, the First Parish retaining the rest. Each was a territorial parish. The Scarboro history tells of the ministers and that they were engaged and paid by the town in the fashion everywhere then in vogue. Church rates were considered by all, except a few Baptists and Quakers, as a regular and proper part of the general tax assessment.

Parson Elvins married the widow of Rev. Samuel Willard of Biddeford and she brought her children to the Scarboro parsonge. One of these children, Joseph Willard, became President of Harvard, so it was said that Dunstan furnished a President for Harvard College. The good and honored parson died Aug. 12, 1776, after a pastorate of thirty-two years. The war of the Revolution had then begun and the Scarboro people were aroused to great effort. The war news was announced each Sunday from the meeting-house steps. Everybody had volunteered for the siege of Boston during the preceding Winter, and it was said that Scarboro men were in the van of Washington's army at the entry of the British evacuation.

The successor of Mr. Elvins was Rev. Benjamin Chadwick, a graduate of Harvard, Class of 1770, who had married Eunice Willard, the step-daughter of Parson Elvins. He was ordained

PROUTS NECK ON THE OCEAN FRONT

THE CHURCHES AND PARISHES

in December, 1776. Mr. Chadwick was a scholarly and refined man but not of vigorous physique. He filled the pulpit acceptably for eighteen years. In 1795, when religious controversies were growing hot and the orthodox church was becoming an object for political attack and his influence specially needed, the good parson became mildly insane and an invalid and retired from the ministry. The illness and feebleness of the pastor left the First Parish practically without a guide. Had he been a vigorous man, it is not unlikely that they would have kept together like the Black Point Church.

Mr. Chadwick lived in the house still called the Chadwick house, adjoining the Dunstan school-house lot, and near the junction of the Old Orchard Railroad with the main line. Parson Chadwick is still remembered as a gentle, lovable man. He had three daughters—Mary, Abigail and Sophia—who lived together at the old homestead until about 1860. They were old-fashioned, gentle ladies who eked out a living by teaching private schools and sewing schools at the house left them by their father, until they became old. Sophia had been blind for a long time. The two last died within a week of each other. Rev. Henry G. Storer and Aunt Gracy Coolbroth gave them particular care. Mr. Chadwick had a fine library and when the Chadwick girls, who had given their property to Joe Milliken to take care of them, died the whole library was sold to a rag peddler, as Milliken exultingly said, "for five cents a pound, kivers and all."

After the dismissal of Mr. Chadwick the Second Parish Church for five years had no settled minister. In 1800 a large new meeting-house was erected about a mile above Dunstan upon a conspicuous lot on the Westerly side of the Broad Turn Road. The change of location was for the purpose of accommodating the Over the River members. The same year, 1800, Rev. Nathan Tilton was ordained as minister of the church.

His house is still standing at the top of the hill on the Northeast side of the road. Mr. Tilton was a Harvard graduate and belonged to the liberal Unitarian wing of the Congregational Church as distinguished from the evangelical membership of the Jonathan Edwards type, but his heterodoxy was satisfactory to none. The liberals became Universalists and the Orthodox turned to Methodism. The large congregations that filled the Tilton meeting-house in its early and pretentious days gradually fell away. Parson Tilton preached to dwindling congregations and after a while became considerably deaf, and in 1827 resigned as pastor. He had a good farm across the road from the meeting-house and had an orchard of mulberry trees for raising silk worms. There he lived until he died in 1851. He had quite a family of children, was interested in educational matters and was an esteemed and good citizen.

After him in 1829 came Rev. Moses Sawyer who remained a couple of years, and then the old church died of inanition. The once handsome and conspicuous Tilton meeting-house stood for a long time vacant and dilapidated, a discreditable wreck. The parish itself became only a memory. I have never been able to learn what became of its old parish record book, if any there was, but the Second Parish Church ministerial records are in the vault of the Maine Historical Society.

The doctrinal rift in the old Congregational churches of which the Second Parish furnishes an example, was a source of weakness, but the political controversy which arose at about the same time was still more disastrous. The subject was fresh in the memory of my grandfather even in his old age and is worthy of a chapter by itself.

XXII

How the Old Orthodox Church Became Unpopular

XXII

HOW THE OLD ORTHODOX CHURCH BECAME UNPOPULAR

FROM the earliest period there was a so-called liberal element of no inconsiderable proportions in the Puritan Church. It was this which aroused the Anne Hutchinson revival in which was preached the necessity for "a covenant of grace," meaning spiritual religion as distinguished from a "covenant of works," a term applied to mere church membership with devout living. The influence of Harvard College with its output of ministers tended towards liberalism. In 1734 there began at Northampton, Mass., under the ministry of Jonathan Edwards a religious revival which developed great proportions and extended influence, so that it is still called The Great Awakening. George Whitefield came from England, made a tour of New England and preached to immense audiences. He held, as has been said, a meeting in Dunstan in 1735. This Great Awakening had its effect in Scarboro. The Black Point, First Parish, Church adhered strictly to the Edwards evangelical orthodoxy, but the tide of liberalism had, after a while, its part in the disruption of the Second Parish Dunstan Church.

The principal cause of the change in the popular attitude towards the old Congregational Church was due to the natural alteration of conditions as the country grew older. The early settlements in New England, including those in Maine, were of religious character. After the Massachusetts occupation, the church and the common school were made fundamental parts of their system. Both were regarded as public institutions, to be supported out of the funds raised for public purposes by taxation. The Puritan idea was to have the churches entirely free in action and creed, but without the power to own and control establishments and lands as was the case in the old countries. Under their system, therefore, the people in the towns and incorporated parishes owned and controlled the buildings and properties used by the churches, while each church, though it could not hold property, made its own creed or declaration of faith and covenant. The ministers, like the teachers, were employed and paid by authority of the town. For about a century and a half this system went on with little open objection, except from a few scattering Baptists and Quakers, who protested against being compelled to pay for preaching in which they did not believe. There was for the churches no means of support outside of the action of the people in their town meetings. With the Revolution there came a weakening of the old doctrinal beliefs, and this was commonly attributed to the influence of the infidel doctrines then popular in France. The coarse criticism of Thomas Paine and his school seemed contrary to good morals.

During the Revolutionary period the old churches had made a most creditable record in behalf of patriotism. After the Revolution the colonies became states, and each adopted a constitution as the fundamental of its organization. The feeling was quite general that the churches, which had so largely determined the character of the new nation, should be made secure against harm from hostile legislation. Accordingly Massachusetts, of which Maine since 1691 had been a component part, by a great majority incorporated in its new constitution, in spite of vigorous but futile objection, a drastic provision making compulsory the support of churches by taxation. All the other states, except Rhode Island, did the same thing. The financial maintenance of churches, which before had depended upon the voluntary act of the maporlty of voters in town meetings, then became compulsory. Energetic objection developed at once. The constitutional provision made no distinction in favor of any denomination but, because nearly all

THE OLD ORTHODOX CHURCH 159

churches were orthodox, they were regarded as the real beneficiaries, and they became the storm center. As opposition increased they were railed at almost as robbers, and upon their part they made retort that they were in fact the protectors of the community against the forces of infidelity and sin and the defenders of righteousness. The amendment of the state constitution by removing the obnoxious clause became a burning issue. With the supporters of the churches it was a matter of conscience. They felt that there could be no reason for the elimination of the constitutional provision except to accomplish the overthrow of religion. The orthodox church people were mostly Federalists.

At first it was largely the Baptists who led the opposition with their plea for soul liberty. Others followed with protest against making the orthodox, or "standing order" as it was called, a state church. There seemed to be reason in this, for the Congregationalists, though having no legal preferment, outnumbered all the rest. The intensity of feeling aroused was something like that which animated the temperance people of Maine when it was proposed to remove the prohibitory amendment from the State constitution. Soon it became a contest on the one side between the Orthodox, or Standing Order, church and its supporters, who as they believed were the defenders of religion and morality, and on the other side those who advocated, as they said, voluntary and independent freedom of conscience.

I can remember Uncle George Boothby, an aged and peculiar religious exhorter of the "Come Outer" type, visiting my grandfather. He wore a full beard and allowed no one to address him as Mr. Boothby, saying "Call no man Master or Rabbi." As if the contest were still pending he declaimed loudly with the energy of long ago, about the Orthodox priests who robbed the widow of her pig and the poor man of his cow by Sheriff sales.

The constitutional provision soon became a troublesome element in politics as well as in the old standing order churches. Through the advocacy of Jefferson the statute for Religious Freedom had in 1786 been enacted in Virginia, a state which originally had placed in its constitution a provision for church support by taxation more positive than that of Massachusetts. The Federalist party quite generally upheld the proposition for compulsory church support. The Democratic-Republicans, as the Democratic party was then called, quite strongly opposed. With this ferment of opinion in existence, Rev. Nathan Tilton, a Harvard College Unitarian and a dissenter from the orthodox creed was, as before stated, in 1800 ordained as minister of the Second Parish Church.

The Baptists had long been opponents of the standing order Congregationalists. A Methodist society was organized at Dunstan in 1802 and the next year it was incorporated by the Massachusetts General Court. Rev. Asa Heath was the first minister. They had made little progress since John Wesley came to this country in 1735, but now they sprung into great prominence and activity. The Universalists, who had existed in a feeble way, developed at the commencement of the century with the zealous advocacy of Rev. Hosea Ballou, an earnest and aggressive growth. The Baptist churches increased in numbers and in membership. After 1805 the Unitarians of the Harvard School quite generally split off from the old church. Others became independents. Factions appeared as groups of "Come Outers" as they were called. Free thinkers and open infidels were much in evidence. My grandfather said every Baptist, Methodist and Universalist was reckoned politically as a Democrat as a matter of course, while practically every orthodox was a Federalist. The Eastern Argus became known as the Scarboro Bible. In 1814 when the charter of the Bangor Theological Seminary was granted it was, for political reasons, camouflaged and was named the Maine Charity School.

THE OLD ORTHODOX CHURCH 161

The theology of Mr. Tilton was satisfactory to none of the factions. How heavily the new Methodist Society at Dunstan drew upon the old Second Parish Church is shown by the statement that it soon had a congregation of some two hundred persons. When it had absorbed most of the orthodox membership the feeling between the two societies began and continued to be exceedingly bitter. It was said that the ministers would not recognize each other.

Mr. Coolbroth was sure that, before the turnpike road was laid out across the common lot, the Second Parish built and occupied a new house on the location where the Methodist church now stands, and that it became disused when the Broad Turn building, the Tilton Meeting-House, was erected and, in spite of opposition, was sold to the Methodists. It was much smaller than the old two-story structure, on the original meeting-house lot, built by the town. About 1839 this was remodelled and a new roof placed over the old one.

At Scarboro Corner a Universalist Society was established with a church of its own, which was joined by most of the Over the River people. The Baptist Church at Eight Corners, called the John Burghy or "Buggy" meeting-house, within the limits of the First Parish, and another Baptist Church at "Bobadil," now South Gorham, each made heavy drafts upon the old Scarboro parishes, even before church support by taxation was abolished. A Baptist Society was organized near Prouts Neck having a meeting-house Southwest of Moore's Brook. Independent ministers held meetings in school-houses.

Massachusetts in its constitutional convention in 1817 refused to change the obnoxious compulsion for church support by taxation, but when Maine became a state in 1820 and adopted a constitution of its own, a provision was inserted, largely through the advocacy of William King, born at Dunstan Landing, the first Governor, prohibiting the support of any churches by other than voluntary methods. This ended the legal phase of the controversy and proved to be a wise arrangement for both people and churches.

It was by reason of so much diversity of opinion that the Second Parish Church became disintegrated. Parson Benjamin Chadwick was an incapacitated invalid. Parson Nathan Tilton was an able minister and much respected, but his religious opinions found small response. The Tilton meeting-house, the finest of the church structures, after being vacant and forlorn for years was, about 1853, sold by somebody to Daniel Harmon who used the material for construction of his barn at Beech Ridge. This barn is still standing. The Second Parish had some quite valuable marsh lands which later were turned over to the Methodist Society. It had also some other properties that became abandoned and ownerless. The remnant of the old orthodox meeting-house lot at Dunstan had various claimants and was recently taken by the town under condemnation proceedings for the soldiers' monument. Thus the old Second Parish and its church became only reminiscences of the good old times.

My grandfather told of the bitterness of the denominational strife which in some cases even separated families. He felt that his own Congregational church had abandoned him. He was a Jeffersonian Democrat and hated the old "Feds" as he called them, but he could not agree with the Methodists and he had no use for the Universalists, so he with some other quite prominent people, withdrew from the controversy and enjoyed his religion by himself.

The church quarrel had much to do with making the town strongly Democratic. The fanciful story is told that, at a town election, there was discovered in the box a Federalist ballot and that the Moderator held it up and said, "There appears to be a Federalist vote here, does any one own up to it?" No one replying he added, "It must be a mistake, throw it out." This was, of course, merely a resentful jest, as the town had always a sturdy minority of Federalists and then of their successors, the Whigs and the Republicans.

XXIII

Schools and Educational System

XXIII

SCHOOLS AND EDUCATIONAL SYSTEM

MY grandfather said that his own opportunities for education were small. He lived at West Concord which was several miles from "the street," as he called the part which is now Concord City proper. The terms of school in his father's rather remote district were short and irregular. His school attendance covered only a few months in all, yet he was a great reader and a good penman and was particularly expert at figures. He once gave me the following example of his mathematical problems:

If twenty dogs for thirty groats
Go forty weeks to grass,
How many hounds for fifty crowns
Can winter in that place?

He volunteered the information that a groat was an old English coin worth four pence, and a crown had the value of five shillings, also that the winter meant the three calendar months. It will be seen that this test of scholarship came before Thomas Jefferson had suggested our present decimal currency.

In those days the family was regarded as the unit. The husband's part and the wife's part in the mutual relation were more clearly defined than now. The husband's province, speaking generally, was out of doors, while the house and the home circle and the oversight of the family were more especially the mother's domain. As the church was of first importance she trained the young children in saying their prayers and in the catechism, and necessarily taught them reading and deportment and the rudiments of education.

Each school district was a separate legal organization within the town, and owned and cared for its own properties. The districts differed in population and extent. The school-house was built by levying a tax upon the property within the limits of the school district, and each had its agent who engaged the teachers and cared for the school accommodations. Consequently, the larger and more populous districts had longer and better schools than those with a smaller number of pupils. The general idea applicable to popular education was simple. It was regarded as a public duty to give to every child an education in the branches of knowledge requisite for general business transactions. Reading, writing, arithmetic and the so-called common branches were taught to all. The person who could not read and write was looked down upon as an object to be spoken of with contempt. It was not, however, considered to be the province of the people to carry education beyond the curriculum of these schools which opened their doors to every child whether rich or poor.

With the common school education the duty of the public to the rising generation ended. The average of the boys and girls were considered to be then well enough equipped, and if any wished to go further they were then considered to be qualified to do so at their own option and expense. In order that there might be opportunity for those who desired higher education, numerous academies were erected and endowed by private effort. These higher schools exerted a marked influence especially in the academy towns where they were located. The academies were regarded as an annex of the common school system and the constitution of Maine adopted in 1820 made it the duty of the legislature to help them, although they were wholly under private control. Most of them from time to time received assistance from the state. These academies fitted their students for the colleges, which were also under private government. Both girls and boys went commonly to the academies, but there were no colleges for women. There was, in fact, no demand for women's colleges. They then taught

SCHOOLS AND EDUCATIONAL SYSTEM 169

little beside Greek, Latin, Hebrew, Mathematics, Theology and some abstract sciences, and were suited primarily for professional men. For such studies women generally, and most men also, had no use and the average individual had little interest in them.

From the time of the Revolution there were in most communities men and women who made teaching in the common schools a part of their regular business. The winter schools were universally kept by men, and it was not uncommon to find in them grown-up scholars past the age of twenty-one. The summer terms had women teachers, many of them also of marked ability. All the colleges had long winter vacations so as to allow their students to go out and teach in the common schools. There was little attempt at classification of scholars and, though instructed in classes, each individual might go on independently to the limit of his ability, and the teacher was expected to help him in his separate studies. I myself had in a common school at the same time children learning the alphabet and a boy fitting for college.

In the locality where my grandfather lived there were notable teachers who kept school winters. Among them were Ira C. Doe, Henry Simpson, Granville McKenny, Robert McLaughlin, William Moulton, George H. Boothby, Maria Libby, Lucy Hunnewell, Statira Staples and others, all of high character and large ability. Almost universally men taught the winter schools and women the summer schools. My father, Freedom Moulton, was for years a teacher and my mother, Shuah C. Carter, also taught, as likewise did every one of their children.

The old Dunstan district was very large, extending from the Stuart neighborhood, some two miles west from the schoolhouse, to the limit of the marshes on the East. Scholars from a distance took their dinners with them and stayed at noon. This district was, until after the strip was set off to Saco, financially able to maintain a year-round school with a man for teacher both winter and summer. It was very nearly of academic grade and had in its curriculum Latin, Algebra, Chemistry, Physics, called Philosophy, and other studies quite beyond the common school course.

Mr. J. F. Coolbroth remembered well the old teachers, "Brisk wielders of the birch and rule." He spoke of Jonathan Coolbroth, who left a fine record there. The first teacher whose school he attended, he said, was Ezra Carter, my grandfather's son, who afterwards was a bookseller in Portland in the old firm of Sanborn & Carter and became an Alderman and Collector of the Port of Portland. His next teacher was Liberty Bacon, a son, I think, of old Doctor Alvan Bacon. Then came Ilus Fabyan Carter and after him Freedom Moulton taught the school for several years.

The school-house was a large one-story building, without paint on outside or inside. Within were rows of seats upon the right and left, with floor space between and the Master's desk opposite the entrance door where he could see all that was going on. The boys occupied the seats at the left hand of the teacher, the girls facing them upon the right. The school-house lately abandoned was built upon the site of the old one about 1860 and was, when built, the finest in the town. Thornton Academy in Saco had a large patronage from Scarboro until the Academy building was burned in 1848 and the old and prosperous academy in Gorham also had many students from this town.

The examination of the teachers for certificates and the supervision of the schools was in the hands of a Superintending School Committee of three, elected by the town. One at least of the committee men was expected to visit each school at least twice each term, and his dignified visitation and his speech was an event of importance to teacher and scholars. Each member of the committee received a salary of ten to fifteen dollars a year.

SCHOOLS AND EDUCATIONAL SYSTEM 171

In the smaller districts the school money was helped out by the families taking turns in boarding the teacher. This course of "boarding round" was in general not unsatisfactory, as each entertainer took pride in caring for the master or mistress so as to show up well with others. The Dunstan school which I attended by no means limited its scope to reading, writing and arithmetic. One of the teachers, a medical student, had classes in chemistry and in anatomy. Another teacher was a land surveyor and he gave instruction in his professional line and in higher mathematics. In this school I got a pretty good start in Latin, Algebra, Bookkeeping and other things, and a drill in history and geography that has remained with me ever since. The spelling schools and school exhibitions with declamations, dialogues and singing were great attractions. The old common schools in some respects gave more ample education than those of later date, for the ambitious scholar could generally take whatever studies he desired in addition to the regular, required branches. The boys built the fires and sawed the wood and did the janitor work by turns and the girls upon their part kept the school-room tidy. Reading in the New Testament was always a part of the opening exercises.

In order to have population sufficient for a really good school it was necessary for some to go a long way, and this fact sometimes made trouble about the location of the school-house. The "setting off" of the strip to Saco in 1841 was promoted by the desire of the Stuart neighborhood to have more convenient school privileges, and the annexation of a portion of Scarboro to Gorham about 1862, was wholly occasioned by disagreement concerning the place for the school building. All in all, the old "deestrict school" did its work well. It came close to the people who rightly regarded it as a fundamental part of their common life. The Bible and the spelling-book were and still are the primal sources of that individual liberty and individual opportunity which have developed what we call Americanism. The schools and communities, it should be remembered, were made local by lack of the easy communication and intercourse which came afterwards with the railroads and telegraph and newspapers.

XXIV

Social Customs and Neighborhood Affairs

XXIV

SOCIAL CUSTOMS AND NEIGHBORHOOD AFFAIRS

PEOPLE of the present day are apt to consider that the old days were times of isolation and that they were lacking in the comforts of life. It does not appear that such was ever the case. Even the pioneer period had the robust pleasures of hunting, fishing and plentiful harvests and the women and children enjoyed the opportunities and the homely luxuries that came from freedom from old-world restraint. Food supplies were varied and abundant. The settlers easily raised sufficient for their families. They cared nothing about markets, for there were none. Indian corn was the chief reliance and the golden ears held together by their braided husks in long traces were the pride of the husbandmen. The sounding flails with rhythmic beat separated the grain from the straw, which also was serviceable in many ways. The supplies could be bartered at the trading stations for English or West India goods and the luxuries of the period.

Among the earliest structures were the grist-mills, and the old circular mill-stones were to be found everywhere along the river banks until Summer visitors gathered them up for adornment of their cottage grounds and stone walls. Fulling-mills came later for dressing the cloth from the housewives' looms. Game abounded in the forests. The wild pigeons in their season came regularly in flocks of countless numbers, and the sea fowl had not learned the fear of man. Fish of all kinds were most plentiful in the streams and in the bays. Old traditions tell of the surface fish piled in windrows along the shore after Easterly storms. The cattle could care for themselves in the open and the commons in Summer, and the marshes and mowing fields supplied their Winter food. Swine roamed somewhat at large, but they and the sheep were menaced by wolves so that they were taken to islands for safety. For this reason the name Hog Island is common.

The climate in their English homes is modified by the Gulf Stream so that Summers there are cool and Winters mild, but they soon got used to the extreme changes of temperature here and enjoyed the heat and the bracing cold. Fuel was free for the cutting and the roaring blaze in the wide fire-places and the candles of bayberry and tallow gave opportunity for story telling and sport. There was mutual and general acquaintance among the settlers. For about two generations there was peace and good-will with the aboriginal people, and then came on the strenuous days of the Indian and the French wars. Men and women lived through these times, except when driven away, with the gallantry of sportsmen and the hardihood of pioneers. When forced to leave their homes the attractiveness of the place each time brought them back.

The old colony times so called, reckoned from the settlement beginnings to the Revolutionary War, covered a period longer than we are apt to consider—nearly a century and a half, the estimated life-time of five generations. All the while independent Americanism was being developed. The Folk lore of the Colonial days shows no trace of melancholy and no complaint of poverty or hardship.

During the Revolutionary War this was an exposed locality. The sea routes and the fisheries were then made dangerous by the British cruisers who captured every floating craft that they could catch. The muster rolls show the names of many Scarboro men in the Continental Army. Others were engaged in the warlike expeditions and in the aggregations of the minute men. At the siege of Boston tradition says that every ablebodied man in the town was there. In Washington's army during the terrible Winter at Valley Forge, Maine had the largest proportion of any of the provinces, comprising more than one-tenth of his whole command.

SOCIAL CUSTOMS

Prior to the Revolution we hear of the frequent frolics and jolly times. David Ring's tavern on the Southwest side of the Black Point highway, opposite the old Church and adjoining the Clay Pits road, was a famous resort. Captain David was a good churchman and he evidently knew also how to keep a hotel. Willis tells of a quality party there from Falmouth and Scarboro being marooned for ten days by an extraordinary snow storm and how the guests enjoyed the time of their lives. Eliza Southgate in her "Girl's Life Eighty Years Ago" describes the frequent parties and gatherings at Dunstan.

In those days people had not assembled themselves in cities and each country district developed its own social resources. My grandfather, who came upon the scene in about the year 1800, could tell tales of the former days as well as of his own. Evidently there was a good deal of "quality" feeling and family pride, as Hawthorne indicates, in his New England reminiscences, and there was foppish and extravagant dressing upon the part of some men and women. The Methodists frowned severely upon this kind of frivolity and the worldliness of the "Standing Order," and particularly upon dancing. The expression "Cards and dice are the devil's device" was in frequent use.

From the personal acquaintance and traditional knowledge of the old gentleman it appears that the social intercourse of the New England people was formerly far more intimate than it is in the more active and self-centered present. In the absence of quick and easy communication each community was compelled to depend upon its own resources. The railroads, the telegraph, the traction cars, the automobiles and the newspapers have made very great changes. Formerly the churches were not only the religious centers but were also sources of intellectual and social entertainment. The person who did not go to meeting became a recluse and lost connection with the outside world. The churches had their conferences and conventions and these were always matters of consequence. There were gatherings for prayer-meetings at the houses and the church socials and picnic excursions brought together the people, young and old. The church structures were used as public halls for town meetings and general assembly. The small school districts with their annual elections and local business affairs brought educational influence home to all. Every ambitious teacher was desirous of having school exhibitions where the pupils spoke pieces and made display of their attainments. Spelling schools, debating societies and singing schools came in the evenings and were sources of public interest. School-houses were community places of assembly for all kinds of lectures and popular meetings. The temperance movement got a large part of its development from the constant school-house campaigns. The school-room was used quite impartially as a place for speakers to display their eloquence concerning political matters. Itinerant dissenting preachers had their meetings in private houses and in the district school-house.

At harvest time the husking parties were extremely popular events. The neighbors, old and young, were invited to help husk the farmer's Indian corn. The barn would be lighted up with lanterns, as related in Whittier's "Mabel Martin." The great joke was to find a red ear of corn which would give right to the young man who found it to kiss all the girls. The red ear was likely to be treasured up for the next year's planting. The work was followed by a bounteous repast prepared by the women folk and the evening finished out with games and festivities. In the Winter season came sleighing parties when the young men with the best rig and festive nags and jingling strings of bells would take their best girls out for a ride over the frosty snow by moonlight. Commonly there would be a supper at some tavern and often mine host would have a fiddler ready for a jolly country dance. At this part my grandfather would shake his head regretfully.

The frames of the heavily timbered houses and barns required a good deal of help and skill to put them together, and the "raisings" were neighborhood events. When the carefully measured timbers had been raised and fitted into their proper places and the last wooden holding pin had been driven, the skeleton structure would be ready for its outer covering of boards and the joiners' work. Then the master builder from his high perch would call "Here's a good frame and deserves a good name, what shall we call it?" Someone would suggest a name and the job was declared finished. The work being done, there would ensue a series of athletic festivities. Wrestling matches were commonly the most prominent. The women would have ready a hearty repast of baked beans, doughnuts, mince pie, coffee, cider and other fixings. The raising of an ordinary building frame with the attendant sports would consume half a day at least.

The women upon their part would have their quilting parties and sewing circles, finishing up with the inevitable repast, conversation and games. The kissing games were enjoyed by the young folks but were not well approved by their elders. The entertainments would break up generally upon the stroke of nine o'clock and the young men would see the girls home. The selection of the home-going partners often called for a good deal of tact. A jesting story tells of a dull young man and a bashful girl. All others had left and they perforce had to go together. He walked upon one side of the road and she upon the other. He broke the silence by saying, "Don't you ever tell, Hannah, that I went home with you," and she replied, "No, Jonas, I surely won't, I'm as much ashamed of it as you be."

In the long winter evenings families would have private parties and sociables with invited guests in numbers limited only by the size of the house. If not too cold the young people would often adjourn to the barn where the wide floor gave opportunity for dancing, but always the somewhat staid, old-fashioned folk would feel shocked at such amusement, which many regarded as really sinful. The participants had to take the chance of being called up before the church authorities and disciplined for their questionable conduct. In the quiet season almost anything would serve as an excuse for getting together.

The breaking out of the roads in winter was always a voluntary proceeding. A substantial string of oxen would be attached to a long sled with a log chained crosswise behind, and all the men and boys who could get the chance would pile on to weight down the sled and shovel away the big drifts. All desired to have a part.

After the Revolutionary War, the trainings made gala days for musters of the militia from several towns together. Each young man was required to appear "armed and equipped as the law directs" and joyfully obeyed the summons. There were rival companies who furnished their own guns, and uniforms, and "string bean" battalions dressed in every-day wear. These military displays were extremely popular and drew crowds of visitors. From them came a great crop of colonels, majors, captains and other titles. The actual training evidently did not amount to much, as the war of 1812 found the country in a wretched condition of unpreparedness. These annual musters continued until about the time of the Civil War.

On all these occasions the women turned out as freely as the men, pleased with the opportunity to display their gowns and ribbons and to provide the needed refreshments. There was never a time when the women did not have their full share in all the events public and private. The wives and mothers were then more influential in the home affairs than they are now. The mother had principal charge of the children and the home, and it was her duty to teach the young ones their catechism and the rudiments of education. I once heard a modern woman say that if her husband should refer to her as "my woman," as they used to do, she would leave him. She did not know that it was also the custom for the wife lovingly to call her husband "my man" as a token of affection.

The farmers frequently "swapped work" with each other, receiving payment with labor in return. It was good form for girls of excellent families to be employed as "help" for their neighbors. Capable women were ready to assist in cases of sickness or trouble without charge, and among them were capable midwives. The "help," as a matter of course, sat at the same table with their employers and took part as equals in family gatherings.

The old gentleman never got quite used to the decimal system of currency established in 1792. He often spoke of fractions of the dollar in shillings—six shillings to the dollar—and thought four and sixpence good pay for a day's work. He felt sure that in the old days of democratic simplicity and well-to-do comfort the people got rather more of happiness and contentment in their lives than is obtained by their descendants in the more hurried and cultivated times in which we live.

XXV

The Proprietors of Scarborough

XXV

THE PROPRIETORS OF SCARBOROUGH

AN ancient vellum-covered book now reposing in the vault of the Maine Historical Society is called the Book of the Proprietors of Scarborough. Ebenezer Libby, who lived at Oak Hill on a road leading from the Portland and Saco highway to and across the Eastern Railroad, scrupulously retained the custody of this volume as a family keepsake during his long life-time. His father Samuel Libby was reputed to have been the last clerk of the "Proprietors," and his son Eben S. Libby after his decease retained the heirloom for a long time, and finally deposited it for safe keeping in the Historical Society vault. There is a second volume which Mr. Libby still holds, but as whatever local value the books had, has long since been effaced, they remain only as mementos of the early attempt to establish land titles.

The book begins with the record of a meeting held June 22, 1720, by virtue of a warrant directed to Philip Duly, a resident of Scarborough, from Samuel Moody, Esquire, "one of his majesties Justices of ye Peace." This warrant was issued pursuant to application made May 27, 1720 by George Vaughan and eleven other "proprietors." A moderator and clerk were chosen, and it was then voted that the white pine timber on ye town commons be reserved for town use and benefit; that 50 akers of land be resarved for ye minister; that ye proprietors book for records be bought and that meetings shall be called by notice given by ten proprietors. There are then recorded the names of forty-eight proprietors and settlers. Nothing is said of the basis of proprietorship, and those who first assumed to act, themselves admitted others to their membership by major vote. The records of meetings are brief and informal, generally stating that a certain number of "akers" of land were voted to a certain person, mostly without giving bounds and making assignments of land for highways and landings. The town is commonly referred to as a separate organization. The voters sometimes confirm the right of some individual to the place on which he resides, but in general their acts relate to common lands. The volume closed with record of a meeting held Jan. 6, 1765 when it was voted to defend an action of trespass brought against one Milliken, who owned by right of the Proprietors of Scarborough, for cutting lumber, thus showing that their authority to dispose of lands was not free from dispute.

I was privileged to see this well preserved record book in my younger days, but could never find any one who could explain its authority further than to say it contained an account of the early land grants in Scarboro. The conditions which were the basis of these old allotments have passed from even local traditionary explanation, and an inquiry opens up a condition of affairs the importance of which is but little estimated.

This volume is a reminder of the long struggle for possession of Maine and the conflict of land titles there. It makes a curious story. To a considerable extent the conditions here were different from those of any other province. It is a wellknown fact that organized settlements in Maine came only after other localities had become well established. Inquiry into the origin of this old book involves the whole record of early discovery, together with subsequent contentious grants and proprietary disputes. Such consideration requires a recital of the very beginnings, and presents the reasons why the settlement of Maine, whose territory was undoubtedly regarded as the most desirable portion of the Atlantic Coast, was so long delayed. It is of interest to recall and follow the attendant circumstances in consecutive order. A systematic statement of events resembles a dictionary of dates, but like Gladstone's budgets, makes interesting reading.

THE PROPRIETORS OF SCARBOROUGH   187

It is known to all that the voyage of Columbus in 1492 gave to the world the first real suggestion of a Western continent. The region was found to be inhabited, but occupation by those called heathen was regarded as giving no right of ownership or title. The head of the Roman Church, as the vicegerent of the Almighty, promptly assumed the right to dispose of the newly discovered heathen lands. Pope Alexander VI, therefore, by his official bull in 1493 divided the new world, whose geography and extent was not at all understood, between the kings of Portugal and Spain by a division line which was later found to give nearly all of the lands to Spain. This was the basis of the Spanish claim to the continent, and Spanish control of the sea kept others away for about a century. The defeat of the Great Armada in 1588 and the overthrow of her supremacy gave others a chance. Prior to 1603 there was quite certainly no European settlement North of Florida.

The French were first to set up an independent claim to Northern America. Nov. 8, 1603, Henry IV gave to Sieur De Monts a charter of all the country lying between the 40th and 46th parallels, that is to say, from about the latitude of Philadelphia to that of Montreal, by name of Acadia, claiming title by right of discovery and exploration. In 1604 De Monts made an actual though temporary settlement at the mouth of the St. Croix River. The English thereupon awoke, and in April, 1606, James the first issued, upon his part, a grant to two companies, called the Plymouth and the London companies, of the lands from about the latitude of Virginia to the Bay of Chaleur, including the whole territory claimed by the French. Each company sent colonies in 1607, one to Jamestown and the other to the place in Maine at the mouth of the Sagadahoc or Kennebec River now known as Popham Beach. This settlement at Sagadahoc was duly organized, but within a year the governor died and it was abandoned. Yet this was later admitted to have been an actual occupation and a basis for title and ownership.

The exact dates of subsequent grants made by the duly authorized Plymouth corporation as a royal agency, though sometimes indefinite and overlapping, later proved to be of major importance. August 10, 1622, the Council of Plymouth, pursuant to the authority conferred upon it by the English sovereign, gave to Sir Ferdinando Gorges and Captain John Mason a patent of the territory between the Merrimac and the Kennebec rivers. This was construed as a conveyance to them as joint land proprietors. In 1634 Mason and Gorges made a division, Mason taking the portion between the Merrimac and Piscataqua rivers and Gorges receiving in severalty that between the Piscataqua and the Kennebec. But in the meantime in 1630 the Council of Plymouth had made another grant, with knowledge and concurrence of Gorges, of a tract forty miles square between Cape Porpoise and Cape Elizabeth. This was called Lygonia or the Plough Patent, and the legality of its admittedly prior existence afterwards caused most serious controversy.

Disregarding or overlooking this action, however, other apportionments were made in 1631 to Cammock, Trelawney and others. Gorges himself set up an organized establishment at Gorgeana or York. In 1635 the Council of Plymouth abandoned its prerogative and surrendered its charter, and in that connection Gorges received royal confirmation of the Territory of Maine. In 1639 a new and comprehensive grant including governmental powers was made direct from the King himself to Gorges of the Province or Palatinate of Maine, extending from the Piscataqua to the Kennebec, and Gorges was commissioned Governor General of all New England. Then came on the great interruption of the English Revolution, beginning with the meeting of the Long Parliament in 1640 and

THE PROPRIETORS OF SCARBOROUGH 189

followed by the Protectorate of Oliver Cromwell. No land titles were given by Gorges other than leasehold rights to the scattered occupants. In 1643, the Parliament being in full control in England, George Cleeve who had taken up a tract in present Portland went to England, and through his influence Alexander Rigby purchased of the other owners the old Lygonia patent of 1630, and Cleeve was made Governor of that province under title of Deputy President, thus superseding the Gorges proprietorship.

In 1646 the title acquired by Rigby and the appointment of Cleeve were duly confirmed by Parliament. An acknowledgment of the authority of Cleeve appears in the Scarborough town record. In the meantime, beginning about the year 1643, the Massachusetts Puritans had set up claim to the Maine territory by virtue of their own charter. In 1658 they enforced their claim by taking forcible possession. They incorporated townships and Cleeve was compelled to abdicate, after a troubled and tumultuous official term of about fifteen years, during which time he had been harassed by the supporters of both Massachusetts and Gorges. Then came the restoration of Charles II in 1660, and in 1679, after a long occupation and control by Massachusetts, the English Chief Justices reversed the decision of 1646, which gave the territory to Rigby, and decided the patent of 1637, supplemented by the Palatinate patent of 1639 to Gorges, to be still in force. Thereupon the thrifty Puritans of Massachusetts immediately "hasted away" and bought the province from the impecunious heir of Sir Ferdinando.

There was now a complicated state of affairs. Massachusetts had purchased Maine as an independently chartered province. It was no part of their commonwealth. A solution was found by appointing Thomas Danforth President of Maine as a Massachusetts possession. July 26, 1684 Danforth, by legislative authority, conveyed the territory within the bounds of Scarborough, as well as other towns, to trustees for the benefit of the inhabitants, who however were not to own in fee, but must pay annual rental to Massachusetts as proprietor.

Then May 21, 1684, came the entire revocation of the Massachusetts Charter by the English Court of Chancery. The letters patent were thereby in terms "cancelled, vacated and annihilated." This cancellation caused a general and complete upsetting of titles. All former grants by virtue of the colony charter were made void, and all the lands in New England reverted to the possession of the English King. The occupants became mere trespassers or tenants by sufferance without right. Sir Edmund Andros was made royal governor and took charge in arbitrary fashion. The Massachusetts possession was at an end, and all of her doings in Maine were declared invalid. Andros attempted to arrange with settlers upon basis of tenantry, but without results, and there was general confusion.

After four years of rule by divine right and royal will at home and abroad, the tyranny of James II brought about the second English Revolution in 1688, when he was overthrown and William and Mary became the elected sovereigns of England. James went to France, and Louis XIV declared war in his behalf against England. The colonists here gave their hearty support to the new dispensation and Governor Andros was arrested. Conditions were thus favorable and resulted in giving to a new province with new boundaries and new name the Province Charter of 1691, called that of the Province of Massachusetts Bay. This was substantially the same as the old colony charter which had been set aside. The important part to us was that by it the Province of Maine was united with and made a part of the new aggregation and thereby became subject to its laws and statutes.

The royal grant expressed in the Province charter did not give outright ownership of the lands. They were to be held "in free and common soccage," that is by definite rental. There was contained, however, a clause stating that grants and conveyances of lands heretofore made to any town, college or persons were not to be avoided for any want or defect of form; and in the intricate verbiage the word "dispose" appeared among the powers granted. These words by quite forced interpretation were construed as authorizing real ownership, and as being applicable both to the former grants made by Massachusetts of township lands and also, after the union, to the Gorges palatinate and Rigby holdings in Maine. These Maine allotments had been of leasehold rights and nothing more. The unauthorized incorporation of Maine towns by Massachusetts was assumed to have been made valid; but the Danforth deeds of 1684 did not agree with the enactments of the General Court and were a different proposition. It was an almost hopeless complication from a legal point of view.

Though the Province of Maine was united with the stronger commonwealth by the William and Mary charter of 1691, its provisions could make little immediate difference there for the reason that the French and Indians were in almost complete possession. In 1690 they had made conquest of Maine so far South as Wells, and all English settlers North of that place had been driven away. This occupation by the French and Indians, though feebly disputed, remained until the peace of Utrecht in 1713 at the close of Queen Anne's War, though after 1702, settlers had begun to return with additional immigrants. Many never came back. The Scarboro town records, which apparently were only random fragments, afterwards copied into the town book, had been sent to Boston for safe keeping during the period of abandonment. The town organization of 1658, upon which those records were based, had by the overthrow of the colony charter legally gone out of existence. It was not in terms revived, but Dec. 10, 1719, there was a meeting of the "inhabitance" and the record book was then returned and after the long hiatus, township government was resumed as a matter of course. At this meeting of the townsmen, town officials were elected by common consent. The old Massachusetts Colony laws seem to have been followed in these proceedings as if retroactive and applicable to Maine and to individual ownership.

The Massachusetts method had been for the General Court to grant a tract of land or a township to certain individuals by name, constituting them proprietors and tenants in common, and they were given authority to make assignment of lots to separate individuals. A mere act of incorporation, like that of Scarborough in 1658, was not a conveyance of property in the soil. At first township grantees claimed to be actual owners of their grant with right to sell upon their own account, but it was soon decided that they held the legislative conveyance in trust only, to be parcelled out to others who might be added to the settlement. The greater part of the Puritan immigrants had come within a brief period and in large numbers. The towns were not regularly established organizations but were an experiment, and were developed gradually. A municipal organization as we see it, was unknown. Their statutory powers were given tentatively and were enlarged from time to time as conditions changed.

It throws light upon the Scarboro situation to consider the restriction placed upon the suffrage in Massachusetts. Originally none were allowed to vote except the church members who were qualified as freemen, and these were selected and sworn as carefully and rigidly as the jurymen of our day. In 1692, after the granting of the new charter a change was made and a property qualification adopted. This limitation was kept

THE PROPRIETORS OF SCARBOROUGH 193

in force, though relaxed as to Maine. An additional complication arose from the fact that the Gorges province had been purchased as a going concern with its distinct governmental and land ownership provisions.

The Danforth deed of Scarboro in 1684, was a conveyance to certain persons named therein as trustees for the inhabitants of the town and their successors. These recipients were to take not as owners, but as rent payers. This deed of the Gorges interest had also plainly gone into the discard with the abrogation of the charter. Accordingly the powers of the townsmen in their "general meeting" of December 10, 1719, were at least doubtful. Prior to 1691, the right to vote in town meetings anywhere belonged only to "freemen" and in Maine there were none of that class.

The so-called "Proprietors" upon their part apparently acted in their meeting of June 22, 1720, upon the assumption that while the town as such had powers of government they, being in possession, were under the Danforth deed or otherwise the owners of the soil or had right to apportion it. Some were not residents, and must have claimed by virtue of purchase. It is impossible without explanation to say what right they could assert in the common and unoccupied territory.

Their action was apparently in the nature of "a combination." This kind of popular sovereignty was adopted to some extent in Maine in places where the lawful right could not be ascertained, and the public requirements made some form of united action imperative. By both townsmen and proprietors actual occupations were generally recognized as giving ownership.

Inspection of their Book and of the town record indicates that there were at the same time two organizations that assumed to make allotment, but not sales, of land. It is curious to note that there is no mention of conflict, for in Falmouth under like circumstances there was violent controversy between those who claimed the township lands there under separate organizations called The Old Proprietors and the New Proprietors.

It is evident that the incoming settlers whether townsmen or proprietors did not concern themselves greatly with paper titles or legal form. They were face to face, not with a theory but a condition of affairs. They and their fathers had cleared farms and built mills in the most desirable places. They were in actual possession, why were they not the owners and proprietors? We do not often consider that the ownership of soil and the powers of government had been regarded as things distinct and separate. The township of Scarboro in 1658 had its bounds set forth, a name given to it and nothing more. By far the greater part was common land unclaimed and unoccupied. The Danforth deed was for the benefit of the "inhabitance" only, but they assumed that there must be authority somewhere to make regulation. No proprietors had been named for the town land. The presumption favored those who had possessed themselves of lots.

The divine right of an English King and titles by leasehold with unknown landlords were to them only fancies. The attacks of the Indians and the French were things of every-day reality, and they had themselves and their homes to defend and arrange for as best they could. The inhabitants of other later organized towns were called proprietors and acted as such. It was unreasonable for the new people who had come upon their own initiative, to take control; and so they came together in meeting, and bought their book, so as to have a permanent record, and made allotments with general acquiescense, because there was pressing need of some distinguishing and official marks of title.

This book was long regarded with reverence as the record evidence of landholders ownership in the town; and their allotments so made, with occupation and lapse of time, ripened into holdings in fee though, as in the case of the Fabyans and the Millikens and the Alger tract, there was trouble about boundary lines. The courts when appealed to later declared that such proceedings, though wanting in legal authorization, were based upon necessity and common consent and must not be disturbed.

XXVI

Individual Ownership of Land in America

XXVI

INDIVIDUAL OWNERSHIP OF LAND IN AMERICA

THE old Proprietor's Book when its origin and history are unfolded is eloquent in its exposition of the persistent effort to obtain individual land titles in America. Today this kind of holding is universal and a matter of course. We have forgotten that it was a new world idea and contrary to ancient precedent. Nothing of the kind had ever been considered in Europe. There everybody occupied his holding by permission of his feudal demesne lord and sovereign master, the King. This was stated by Coke and Blackstone as the common law. The royal charters were grants to certain loyal subjects in corporate fashion, to hold and manage as the King's representatives for the purpose of promoting orderly settlement of this new and unsurveyed portion of the royal domain. A division among individuals for private ownership was not mentioned. But with the settlers thrown upon their own resources that proposition soon became a thing of absorbing interest. They knew that a direct request to the Sovereign for such concession would be considered an affront, and that it must be brought about by indirect means if at all. The Massachusetts Bay corporators were allowed to extend their organization by adding to their membership, which at first consisted of a Governor, a Lieutenant Governor and so-called assistants eighteen in number, but they did so in almost wholesale fashion by taking in all qualified freemen as additional members. This was not overlooked in England. Barely six years elapsed before proceedings were set on foot to revoke the charter and put a stop to such disregard of kingly prerogative. This would have been promptly done had it not been for foreign wars and domestic complications which demanded all of the attention of the Government at home. The General Court as immigrants came fast, made allotments to sundry individuals of tracts of land as townships or towns. It was first claimed that these grantees were themselves owners in common, but soon it was declared that they were only holders as trustees for the benefit of the incoming settlers as well. Then, in tentative fashion, the towns were authorized to choose certain officers and to exercise certain municipal powers and to allot and dispose of the common land. In this authorization the official freemen only were included as voters, but presently in democratic fashion the people all came together in "general meetings." The corporate growth of the towns went on tentatively and almost furtively. They knew that it was little short of treason to the monarchial instincts of the mother land. The colony statutes were carefully preserved, but for a long time were not compiled in printed form. It required something of research to learn what they were.

This kind of development did not pertain to Maine until after the union. There the matter of land proprietorship was upon an entirely different basis. The royal authority and the royalistic system were unquestioned. The establishment of the Gorges Palatinate province of Maine and the appointment of Sir Ferdinando as Governor General of New England was designed to put an end to the democratic and revolutionary practices of the Southern portion. Prior to the Massachusetts occupation there was no suggestion of individual titles in fee of settlers upon lands in Maine. Those occupying under the Gorges authority were tenants in good old English fashion. When the Lygonia or Rigby proprietorship was substituted it was the same. Gov. George Cleeve was authorized to give and did give leases only. This was contrary to his own inclination, for he when ousted from his Spurwink plantation had refused to retain it as a leasehold, saying he would be tenant to no man in New England. A large part of the reason for submission by Scarboro and Falmouth to the Massachusetts encroachment consisted of desire to obtain the benefit of the individual land system which was in effect there. When Massachusetts later purchased the Province of Maine from the Gorges heir she did not venture to alter the land tenure there. The Danforth deed of 1684 provided for quit rents and not for ownership in fee. When the charters went down in 1684 before the onslaught of James the second, and Governor Edmund Andros took possession of all lands in the King's name, all the provincial land grants were obliterated and a rental system roughly enforced. The English Revolution of 1688 and the forced abdication of James and Andros, his governor, gave the sovereignty to Parliament. By reason of stress of war and French attack it was for the interest of William and Mary to reward and confirm the allegiance of the provincials by giving them a new and liberal charter.

The old Colony Charter which had been abolished by decree of the Court of Chancery had no provisions relating to towns or town governments or individual land titles in fee. The province Charter granted by the new sovereigns was likewise silent in that regard, but it confirmed all grants that had been made by the General Court to persons, towns, villages, colleges and schools, and authorized the General Court to make wholesome and reasonable laws pertaining to the common good and welfare. From these provisions the liberty-loving New Englanders assumed the right to do pretty much as they pleased. The inclusion of Maine in the Province of Massachusetts Bay in 1691 was assumed to carry with it the authority of Massachusetts statutes both old and new. But, after all attempted explanations, it must be said that it is not possible to find definite legal foundation for land titles in Maine, or for township government, for the good reason that there was no such basis established. There was little of technical law about it. It was a time when the needs of the situation and the requirements of the general welfare demanded and controlled action. Scarboro never had any incorporation except that of 1658 which "included (with indefinite bounds) those places formerly called Black Point, Blew Point and Stratton's Island to be henceforth called by the name of Scarborough," extending back eight miles from the sea. The efforts of the French to conquer America did not cease with the peace of 1713. A condition of warfare was kept up continuously until the capture of Quebec in 1759 through the Indians who were mere puppets under French control. The musket as well as the plow was a part of the pioneer's equipment.

Any discussion of individual land titles in America would be grossly inadequate if it did not include much consideration of the tremendous effect of concurrent events in the mother country. The victory of Parliament, the Protectorate of Cromwell and the Revolution of 1688 created there, as has been said, a republic under the guise of royalty. The divine right of kings became a forgotten thing. The progressive tendencies of the American were looked upon with satisfaction by the English Whigs and Liberals. So far as England was concerned no repressive measures were even suggested from the time of the Province charter until the reign of George the third.

By the year 1718 the contests of contending claimants and wars, which for three-quarters of a century had made secure settlements in Maine impossible, had been mostly adjusted. French and Indian hostilities were for a time quieted and the province was a land of desire to which there came a flood tide of immigration. New towns were incorporated fast. The system of distribution of lands by towns and so-called proprietors, which had been invented to fit the necessities of the case, was adopted generally and by common consent. It became the accepted method, though considerable of trouble arose from the assertion of conflicting prior rights under the early grants and occupations, and especially from the uncertain boundaries. Possession and lapse of time with the so-called statutes of rest brought security to land titles and Maine, which had been almost a no-man's land during the long period when the organized colonies were growing into established communities, became a place where settlers might feel secure in the possession of their improvements and homes.

The new world idea of the independent citizen owning real estate in his own right had prevailed. The legality of the action of the proprietors was never approved, but their method was effective. In the old case of Rogers v. Goodwin, 2 Mass. 478, where it was claimed that their conveyances made merely by vote were without authority and void, the Court held such titles good, saying, If it were a new question it might be very difficult to maintain such construction, but even if the practice originated in error, the error is now so common and property rights so generally involved that it must have the force of the law.

XXVII

Three Scarboro Women

XXVII

THREE SCARBORO WOMEN

THE settlement at Scarboro was one of the earliest made on the New England coast. The Pilgrim fathers landed at Plymouth in 1620. The Puritans began their settlement at Boston ten years later. Somewhat earlier than that John Stratton had his trading post upon the islands off the Scarboro shore which still bear his name. In England great interest had awakened for settling the new lands across the sea, and among those who desired to promote the upbuilding here was the Earl of Warwick, of the family to which the great Warwick, called the King Maker, belonged. He had a nephew, Thomas Cammock, and the Earl by reason of his rank and influence, obtained for him a grant of land which included the beautiful peninsula which we know as Prouts Neck.

Cammock took up his abode there in 1631 when Boston was having its beginning and Plymouth had only passed its tenth year. With Cammock came his wife Margaret, a bright and capable woman, and on their little territory they set up a sort of baronial residence and called it Cammock's Neck.

For some twelve years they enjoyed their most attractive home. Then Cammock went on a voyage to the West Indies where he died. By his will he made Margaret for her life-time the sole proprietor of the tract which in its extent included more than two square miles. Thus Madame Cammock, in her own right, became the sole landed proprietor and manager of the Cammock Patent, then called Black Point with its lands and privileges appurtenant. But Margaret, alas! was a woman and preferred a husband rather than the position of an independent proprietor, and so after a brief period, she married Henry Jocelyn, whom her husband had recommended as an adviser and friend. Her new husband held high official positions in the colony while she was queen of the household, and for many years they occupied their fine abode, honored and respected by a very wide circle of acquaintances and friends.

About five years after Thomas and Margaret Cammock had established themselves upon the Neck a company obtained a patent of land upon the easterly side of the Saco River. They were attracted by the sloping hill of Blue Point where it rises from river and shore, and as this was unquestionably east of the Saco River, they disregarded their proper limits and set up their plantation there. In this company which contained names of distinguished old-world families was a young couple, John Jackson and Eleanor, his wife.

Jackson soon sickened and died, but Eleanor was brave and remained with her friends in the settlement. Jonas Bailey, a very thrifty neighbor, was a widower. Mutual sympathy drew the bereaved ones together and presently Mrs. Jackson became Mrs. Jonas Bailey. They were happy in their wedded life for a few years only when Mr. Bailey also passed to the great Beyond, and the good wife was again a widow.

Eleanor was a woman of character and ability, and like many other women of the time, took much interest in public affairs. She obtained from the town a grant of one hundred acres of land and bought additional tracts from Henry Jocelyn and others and became known as one of the largest proprietors of land in the town. She was her own manager and appears upon the record as a planter in her own right. Her later career is unknown, but it is thought that she retained her prominence as a public-spirited business woman until the Indian hostilities disrupted the happy colony.

More than forty years after the settlement in 1631 passed in prosperity and peace when Count Frontenac became Governor of New France, as Canada was then called, and attempted to conquer all of America for France. In 1690 he sent his troops with their Indian allies in overwhelming force to drive the English from Maine, and all of the Scarboro settlers were then forced to leave the place. After a dozen years some came back to try to locate anew their desolated homes. Scarcely had they arrived when the French and Indian war broke out anew and garrison houses were built for places of refuge in case of attack.

Among those who took part in the second settlement was Roger Dearing, who, in 1716, came to Scarboro from Kittery. He purchased from the heirs of Rev. Robert Jordan the "Nonsuch Farm," lately owned by Henry G. Beyer, and his house there was one of the garrison houses. In 1723 the Indians made a sudden attack in the absence of the owner and Mrs. Dearing was killed.

Mr. Dearing married for his second wife Elizabeth Lydston Skillings. After peace was declared they occupied the old homestead. In 1741 Mr. Dearing died, and by his will left a legacy to the Scarboro Church and a legacy to the religious and industrious poor, and all the remainder of his large estate to his well-beloved wife, Elizabeth.

Madame Dearing, as she was called, was a true colonial dame of great dignity and influence. For years she managed with great ability her large estate. In those times slavery was a recognized institution in Maine and elsewhere, and the records tell of her black servant, Hagar, who was married to black Caesar, the servant of Captain Prout. In her life-time she was highly honored and much beloved and her funeral was attended by a great concourse of citizens.

It would be hard to find in all the history of the beginnings of Maine the names of three individuals who, by their lives and character, exerted more influence for good than these three noble women, whose names are still held in honor.

www.ingramcontent.com/pod-product-compliance
Lightning Source LLC
Chambersburg PA
CBHW071437150426
43191CB00008B/1153